ELEMENTARY PRINCIPAL'S HANDBOOK:
New Approaches to Administrative Action

ELEMENTARY PRINCIPAL'S HANDBOOK:
New Approaches
to Administrative Action

Reynold Bean and Harris Clemes

Parker Publishing Company, Inc.
West Nyack, New York

Library of Congress Cataloging in Publication Data

Bean, Reynold
    Elementary principal's handbook.

    Bibliography: p.
    Includes index.
    1. School management and organization--Handbooks,
manuals, etc. 2. Elementary school principals--
Handbooks, manuals, etc. I. Clemes, Harris,
joint author. II. Title.
LB2806.B357   372.1'2'012   77-29123
ISBN 0-13-259473-0

Printed in the United States of America

Dedication–

For Halimah and Maya, who, actually, are very
good administrators.

About the Authors

Reynold Bean is a graduate of the Harvard Graduate School of Education, and has held a wide variety of positions in education. He was a founder and director of an experimental high school, and has maintained an interest in the problems of adolescence as a counselor, as a teacher, and through extensive work with delinquents.

His experience in administration includes work with County Offices of Education, a Family Service Agency, Residential Treatment Center for delinquents, and consultant to school administrators.

He has taught teachers and administrators, and served as consultant to many schools, social agencies, and businesses in areas covered by this Handbook.

Mr. Bean is a Family and Child Counselor, has co-authored manuals for parents and teachers in the education of children, and is associated with the Association for Personal and Organizational Development, an educational consulting firm.

Harris Clemes, Ph.D., is an associate with the Association for Personal and Organizational Development. He is a licensed psychologist and maintains a practice in psychotherapy, in addition to extensive organization development consulting to schools and public service organizations. For many years, he has been an instructor for the University of California in the areas of Conflict Resolution, Visualization, and Raising Self-Esteem of Children. Dr. Clemes has previously been a staff psychologist at Stanford Medical School, and Assistant Professor at Occidental College. For six years he was a Research Associate at the Mental Research Institute, where he designed and conducted research programs in the area of communication, and the assessment of social environments.

Note to the Reader

The names of persons and schools used in the many case examples in this Handbook have been changed to preserve the anonymity of teachers and administrators. In some cases, details have been altered so as to further this intention, without jeopardizing the example which the case illuminates.

The Authors

How This Book Will Help the School Administrator...

"If it were not for some of the people I have to deal with, being a principal would be a great job." An elementary school administrator in California once summed up his feelings in that manner. His concern, shared by most administrators, is the focus of this book.

Dealing with people—teachers, other administrators, parents, and children—is really the chief activity of the elementary administrator. Those who can effectively work with people are "good" administrators. Those who can't, have stresses in their schools and within themselves. This Handbook is a practical and useful reference work for all elementary principals, as well as those central office administrators who need to work closely and effectively with building administrators. By using the procedures described in this book, you will be able to gain a number of important advantages in your school. For example, it will be an invaluable guide if you want . . .

- to see meetings become arenas for *productive* activity
- conflict translated into constructive *action*
- closer teamwork between teachers, parents, and children
- ways to defuse explosive situations
- viable alternatives to the damned if you do, damned if you don't dilemma
- to turn competition into cooperation
- to harness the power of positive self-images
- to improve performance in any school sector

9

10

- techniques that will help you increase staff harmony, productivity, and job satisfaction
- tested, effective solutions to everyday problems
- procedures that will help you gain more satisfaction from your position
- to handle your own "personal stress" more effectively.

If you are like most administrators, your training was probably rather sparse and largely academic in terms of acquiring the tools needed to work with large numbers of people in organizational settings. You have since found that "theories" about dealing with people aren't easy to apply under the day-to-day stresses and time demands on your job. When "push comes to shove," you don't need another theory; you need a practical solution—something that will work for today's problem, and allow you to get on with the business of running a school.

There's a story about the farmer who used old-fashioned, traditional farming methods. One day he was confronted by a modern, scientifically minded agricultural agent. The young man wanted the farmer to adopt some of the new features of the current farming practices, but the farmer was somewhat resistant. "Well, why don't you want to try some of these ideas? They can surely help to improve your yield and make your work easier," the youthful expert implored. The farmer replied: "Son, even though I'm working hard, I'm only doing half as well as I know how. Let me catch up to myself, and then I'll likely try some of your ideas."

School administrators often find themselves in the same position. You know what you ought to be doing, but the "lack of time and resources" often keeps you from doing it. You may have a clear sense of the goal you want to reach, but you may be unsure about the steps that are required to reach it.

This Handbook recognizes that the *main task of the school administrator is to organize people and other resources in such a manner as to get things done. Specifically, to insure an effective educational climate and protect the educational integrity of a school*. Promoting, organizing, monitoring, and evaluating the things that teachers, students, and parents do is your dominating job.

We will include *practical* procedures for dealing with the large number of people-related issues you are likely to face. The broad range of step-by-step procedures will enable you to *do* something about your ordinary and extraordinary problems. Case studies, gleaned from real-life experiences of working administrators, are included in order to demonstrate the application of tested ideas—and the results they can help you achieve.

Many problems with which you are faced involve complex features of human relationships. For this reason, we have cross-referenced sections of the Handbook in order to provide a broad view of a problem, as well as procedures you can use in solving it. Theories are kept to a minimum, and the coordinated references will be helpful to those readers who wish to explore some topics in greater detail.

As an example, in the chapter on Conflict Resolution, you will find cross-references to the sections on Communications, Problem Solving Procedures, Working with Parents, etc. You can use what you need, and come back to the Handbook when new wrinkles occur in old problems.

The table of contents is organized in a way that will make the Handbook more usable to you. Checklists, surveys, and training formats are included which may be used directly from the Handbook, or easily adapted to your own situation. We have always asked ourselves the question, "Will the administrator be able to *use* this?"

The job of being a school administrator doesn't vary much from one school district to another. In all sections of our country, the problems are similar, and the stresses of the job are growing everywhere. As parents become more involved in school affairs, as teachers become more insistent in their demands, and as changing family patterns affect children, the administrator is increasingly called upon to manage the *human resources* of a school community in imaginative and productive ways.

An administrator who has had long experience in a number of schools once put it this way: "What happens to kids in a school is always the result of how adults in that school are getting along. When the parents, teachers, and principal are doing their jobs, the kids will do theirs."

This Handbook will guide you in helping others do their job more effectively. That's your job . . . and each chapter that follows will show you how to do that job in more productive, rewarding ways.

Reynold Bean
Harris Clemes

Acknowledgments

Many people have contributed to this Handbook, especially the hundreds of teachers and administrators with whom we have had the privilege of working. As consultants to schools we have often felt like "messengers," picking up information in one place and taking it to another. We have found that administrators seem to profit most from solutions that other administrators have discovered. In this Handbook, we have attempted to distill their experience. Literally hundreds of years of experience, accumulated by many of our colleagues in schools, have gone into this book. We especially wish to note our gratitude to the administrators and teachers in Santa Cruz County in California, who have been so open and willing to share their experiences with us.

Special acknowledgments are due Jack Wendt of the Santa Cruz County Office of Education, who provided the wherewithal and professional support for our initial research into how schools work. Mrs. Ann Soldo allowed us to work with her and her staff for some time. Many years as a school administrator have not dimmed her interest in learning how to be a better one.

Hamilton Brannan taught us much about elementary school administration. As an elementary administrator, he represents the best in the reasonable and humane application of the ideas described in this Handbook. Our many years of work with him have deeply influenced us. His love for children has demanded that he run his school in a way that best serves them. This, after all, is the goal of good administrative practice.

Robert B. Stone, who is a very good teacher for amateur writers, made this book possible in most concrete ways.

Lastly, Rifka McClure Several and Marilyn Darling spent a great portion of their time for a year going over and over this material. But for them it would not exist.

Reynold Bean
Harris Clemes

Table of Contents

13

ELEMENTARY PRINCIPAL'S HANDBOOK:
New Approaches to Administrative Action

1

How to Evaluate Teacher, Principal, and School Climate

This chapter will describe ways to evaluate your staff's performance, your own performance, and the climate of your school. Evaluation is the most important first step to improving performance. If it is done well, it can open the door to creative and imaginative change.

Evaluation can be used in two ways:

• To make a judgment about one's fitness or adequacy to do a job. In this sense, it becomes a threat or weapon. It measures success or failure by an abstract standard.

• To identify areas of strength and weakness with the intention of reinforcing strengths and providing resources to correct weaknesses. In this sense, it becomes a tool to promote change.

In this chapter, we will propose using evaluation in ways that emphasize the second approach.

1.1 EVALUATING TEACHER PERFORMANCE

There is often considerable stress surrounding this process for both the evaluator (the administrator) and the evaluatee (the teacher). There are a number of reasons why this stress exists:

• The many relationships that an administrator and a teacher have create a cloud of ambiguity around the relationship. The administrator may be a supervisor, friend, "servant" (in that you provide the things the teacher needs), stranger (in the event you don't know each other well), etc. Such ambiguity results in anxiety.

• It may be unclear to what purposes the evaluation will be directed. How will it be used, and by whom?

• There may be little clarity about the standards or criteria to be used in the evaluation. Will it be arbitrary or objective?

• A teacher may believe that her own unique characteristics may not be given adequate weight in the evaluation.

• If the teacher perceives her goals to be different from the administrator's, she will be anxious about the overall "fairness" of the evaluation.

How to deal with these problems and others is discussed in Section 1.14.

1.11 How to Observe the Teacher in the Classroom

Consider how you might feel if you were to be evaluated under the following conditions:

• You and your evaluator did not know each other very well.
• The evaluator was unfamiliar with what you have been doing.
• You didn't know the areas of performance or the criteria that were to be used in the evaluation.
• You were observed briefly on one day, at a time that was not representative of your overall performance.
• You had the impression that the evaluator didn't like you very much.
• The evaluator had little understanding of what your long-range goals were, and didn't know where you were in the process of accomplishing them.

If these things were to occur, you surely would tend to be apprehensive about the evaluation. You might be resentful and resistant to the process, no matter what district policy said.

These conditions occur to some degree between administrators and teachers who are involved in an evaluation.

A number of things can be done to prepare a climate in which evaluations are used as a positive tool to improve performance.

• *Know your teachers.* Developing good relations with teachers requires places and times where you associate with them individually and in groups.

• *Make your presence in classrooms an ordinary occurrence.* Visiting classrooms should not be reserved for special occasions (such as evaluations). The children, as well as teachers, will benefit from your having a sense of what's happening to them. It helps if they become adapted to your presence.

• *Clarify the role you play in helping teachers improve their performance.* When you fulfill your responsibilities by providing resources, promoting training, assessing needs, evaluations become part of a broader process.

• *Share yourself.* Knowing what your opinions, values, and attitudes are helps teachers trust you.

• *Show concern.* Your staff will have confidence in your responsiveness, fairness, and caring, when you have worked with teachers to accomplish their goals, followed through on working out problems, and helped them through difficult personal or professional situations.

• *Make evaluations important.* In many schools, evaluations are done pro-forma. Work with teachers to make evaluations meaningful. In a staff discussion on evaluation, allow staff to share their apprehensions and to suggest procedures.

• *Set up a staff committee on evaluations.* When staff have the opportunity to participate in planning and monitoring evaluation procedures, their interest in and commitment to the process grow.

1.111 Types of behavior to be evaluated

1. A.

If the district's evaluation process is adequate for the purpose of improving performance, and if teachers and administrators are comfortable with it, then it may suffice as the approach to use. Sometimes, though, you may be given the forms, but an effective process for completing the task is not clarified. You need to be confident about what it is that you ought to be observing. The following are factors that have been shown to be important in teacher performance and productivity.

A. Warmth
   a. The teacher provides positive reinforcement through praise, and pays close attention to what children say.
   b. The teacher makes physical contact with children by holding hands, hugging, touching, etc.—in ways appropriate to age and sex.
   c. The teacher uses humor frequently, especially in ways that do not disparage or shame children.
   d. The teacher makes frequent contact with individual children by a touch, a comment, eye contact, smiles, etc.
   e. The teacher adjusts the style of contact, taking into account differences among children.
B. Clarity in communication
   a. The teacher gives directions that are understandable to children.
   b. The teacher makes clear, prior to a new task, what is going to happen, and how it should be done.
   c. The teacher makes frequent checks for feedback from children, asking them to repeat what they heard her say, clarifying that they understood, and seeks their opinions on events in the classroom.
   d. When the teacher asks a question, she leaves sufficient time for children to respond to her.

     e. When children respond, the teacher makes frequent use of paraphrasing to indicate her comprehension of what the child has said.

C. Classroom management

     a. Consequences for misbehavior are clarified to individuals and the class, and follow-through occurs.

     b. The teacher makes minimal use of threats when attempting to manage children.

     c. The classroom rules are clear to children, and frequently referred to.

     d. The noise level of the classroom is monitored by the teacher, and varies according to the activity.

     e. The teacher gets the class's attention when she requires it, and commands the children's interest in what she does and says.

D. Physical arrangements

     a. There is physical evidence of current activities that reinforce directives and the main principles being taught.

     b. The teacher maintains a standard of neatness, which is appropriate to the task at hand, and furthers the goals of the activity.

     c. The decorations and displays in the classroom stimulate interest and attention.

     d. The arrangement of desks and tables makes effective use of space, promotes effective grouping of children, and insures safety.

     e. Materials are easily accessible to children.

E. Productivity

     a. The teacher completes activities in the time and sequence that was defined.

     b. The teacher is able to specify short- and long-range goals, objectives, and activities (relative to the school's policies and curriculum), and is on target in accomplishing them.

     c. When teaching a lesson, the teacher has all materials required, in sufficient quantity to complete the task.

     d. There is available a variety of materials that serve the needs of children who are working at various levels of competence.

     e. The teacher has procedures that identify various competence levels.

     f. Administrative requirements are completed by the teacher on time, and at an appropriate standard.

1.112　Observation checklists

When observing teachers for evaluation, it is best if the procedure takes into consideration the following issues:

• What is to be observed should be as concrete, specific, and objective as possible. One cannot observe a teacher's "attitude" but can observe behaviors that demonstrate an attitude.

• A list of behaviors can be communicated to teachers before the evaluation (they can have a hand in preparing it, see Section 1.11), and can be used as an objective reference in the evaluation discussion (Section 1.142).

• An overall impression is less useful in helping teachers improve performance, than is reference to specific acts.

• A method for tabulating what you see is needed. Sometimes a teacher's style is not to your taste, even though she may be performing quite adequately. Avoid allowing evaluations to be based on impressions.

In order to accomplish the above, some type of behavioral checklist will be helpful. If you wish to use the behaviors that were specified in the previous section, they can be a start in creating such a checklist.

The observed behaviors should, insofar as possible, relate to the teacher's and school's goals. For instance, if a major project or program at the school is concerned with reading improvement, items on the checklist should illuminate the teacher's performance in that area. If a major goal of the school is to improve children's self-esteem, the teacher's performance in doing so should be evaluated. If the teacher is developing an "open-classroom" approach, specific criteria for that program should be included on the checklist.

A further virtue of a checklist is that it clarifies to you, the teachers, and others who are involved in evaluation, just what it is that's important in classroom behavior. Such a shared perspective can go a long way toward developing a common view of what "good" teaching means, and can improve the climate within your staff.

The following are some specific recommendations about the construction and use of a behavioral checklist:

• The checklist need not be the same as the final evaluation form. The checklist is only a device to tabulate your observations. It can be summarized on a final document (possibly the district has its own form).

• The checklist should be on one face of one sheet of paper, easily read, so that items can be found quickly.

• As you observe, you can record what you see by checking items, or by having a rating system. A check system means that any time you observe the behavior you check the item. At the end of the observation period you then have a record of what the teacher has done and to what degree. A rating system involves making a summary judgment for each item at the end of the observation, i.e., 1—does frequently, 2—does sometimes, 3—does rarely, 4—not observed. Such a system as proposed here allows you to observe much and tabulate little. Making notes as you go can be time consuming, and you can miss a lot.

• If you use a rating system, you may wish to record your observations after you leave the classroom. It's important to do so immediately, so as not to lose touch with what you saw.

• Do your observation during two or three time segments, at different times on different days, and when the teacher is engaged in various activities. Some teachers get apprehensive if the whole evaluation rests on one observation.

Teachers' energy levels go in cycles; most are better at some times of day than others.

• If you take observations seriously, do not attempt to observe more than two or three teachers concurrently. You will begin to compare (which may be unfair), and you will "overload" your awareness about what you are seeing.

• Items on the checklist should be both positive and negative. For instance, "Touches children in appropriate ways," and "Voice level is often low." Having all items worded similarly creates a "halo" effect, and will influence what you see, whether you are aware of it or not.

1.113   Reducing teacher anxiety during observations

The following are a summary of things you can do in order to reduce the apprehension of teachers who are being evaluated and observed.

• Clarify when and how feedback from the observation will be given. Do it soon after you complete the observations.

• Let teachers know that the evaluation discussion with them will occur before the final evaluation form is completed.

• Let staff know when evaluations are being done. Often staff will become mutually supportive, and teachers can ventilate anxieties to each other.

• Have teachers and children become adapted to your presence in the class through prior visits.

• Have a pre-observation conference with a teacher to discuss the observation, to schedule times (if appropriate), and to hear if there are any special or unusual conditions in the teacher's class, e.g., excessive absences, visitors, new children, special behavior problems, etc. If teachers know that you are willing to take such unusual conditions into consideration, they will be less anxious.

• Anxiety is reduced by increasing control. When teachers feel that they can affect the procedures and outcome of evaluations, they will feel *part of* the process, not *subject to* it.

• If teachers know that you believe that the central purpose of evaluation is to help them improve their performance, a very positive climate can occur.

1.12   Using Children's Performance as Evaluation Criteria

Ultimately, the criteria about whether or not a teacher is effective rest in what happens to children in his or her class—how they act, and the degree to which they learn.

This section will point out how you can use children's behavior as a factor in evaluating teachers.

1.121   Raw data analysis

How much of what children *should* be learning depends on a number of factors, among which are:

- Prior preparation of the children.
- Parents' and teachers' expectations.
- Availability of resources.
- Personal characteristics of the children.
- Teacher performance.
- The reasonableness and clarity of the school's and teachers' goals.

Setting an absolute standard for judging teacher competence based on children's performance in skills tests is subject to endless argument and disagreement. There are always mitigating circumstances. Recognizing this limitation requires using such data as an indication of a teacher's performance, rather than the absolute standard of it.

If your school uses some type of standardized testing of children in academic areas, the scores that any particular class makes on such tests can provide a number of different kinds of information, which can be used in assessing a teacher's performance.

• The average of scores for the class can tell you something about the overall progress of the group.

• The range of scores can tell you about the difficulty the teacher may have in meeting a variety of needs.

• The number and level of low scores can show the need for remediation.

• The number and level of high scores can show the need for enrichment.

All of the above issues can be used in teacher evaluation, in terms of *assessing the way in which a teacher goes about responding to these facts.*

If your school and teachers have specified goals, with derivative objectives in the area of children's academic performance, their progress toward these goals should be measured periodically. This is not only for the purpose of evaluating teachers, but also to have feedback measures of children's progress.

Since expectations (by teachers, parents, *and* children) play such a large role in determining children's productivity, having appropriate goals is the first step in defining acceptable performance levels. Without such goals, it is difficult to evaluate a teacher's performance based on students' progress. (See Chapter 3 on Goals.)

Another criterion for evaluating teacher effectiveness is the extent to which a teacher is aware of, and develops programs for, individual students' levels of competence. You can evaluate a teacher's capability in this regard by making a review of student performance part of the evaluation process. This might involve looking through student folders with the teacher, listening to her views on students, and learning what her objectives are for individuals. One useful method is to select two or three slow students and two or three superior ones for an in-depth review.

1.122   Children's behavior as data

Children's response to the way a teacher handles the class is expressed in their behavior. When a teacher's performance is being evaluated, there are things that can be observed in children's behavior that indicate specific problems the teacher may be experiencing. Every classroom will have some children who act in these ways. In a poorly managed class, the incidence of these behaviors will be excessive, contributing to a general disruption of the learning environment.

A. When a teacher communicates poorly, you will observe the following:
   a. Students will ask questions about assignments excessively, and the questions will be repetitive.
   b. Students will ask each other questions about what to do.
   c. There will be considerable conflict in group activities, i.e., sports at recess, classroom projects.
   d. Students will be slow to start new activities.
B. When a teacher lacks authority and control, you will observe the following:
   a. Students will pay little attention to the teacher's directions.
   b. Students will ignore specific directives to stop doing something.
   c. There will be excessive fighting—physical and verbal—in the class.
   d. Children will argue with the teacher over minor issues.
   e. The class will not quiet down quickly when the teacher requests it to.
C. When the teacher has not clarified standards about appropriate classroom behavior, you will observe the following:
   a. Students will be verbally abusive toward each other.
   b. Students will yell or shout a lot.
   c. The classroom will tend to be messy and sloppy—and so will the students.
   d. There will be a general lack of cooperative behavior.
D. When a teacher lacks organization, you will observe the following:
   a. Students will evidence boredom, by staring into space, playing aimlessly at desks.
   b. Students will wander about the class, without seeming to know what to do.
   c. Students ask questions about where to find things.
E. When a teacher fails to foster independence and share authority, you will observe the following:
   a. Students will cling to the teacher, and want her attention excessively.

  b. Students will continually check with the teacher about what to do.
  c. Students will often seek the teacher's affirmation about their progress.
  d. Students will ask permission for things, even for minor issues.

1.123   Evaluating children's satisfaction with teacher

Education is one area where consumer satisfaction is rarely evaluated. The practice of asking children to evaluate a teacher's performance is not widespread, although some adventurous teachers do elicit such information in formal ways. (We know of one teacher who has designed a report card which children and parents fill out on his performance. You can be sure he gets good grades.)

The degree to which students are satisfied with their teacher is an important factor in their learning and productivity. Furthermore, children who like and respect their teacher will ordinarily feel good about themselves, and the classroom climate will be a positive one.

If your teachers are willing to take the risk of hearing what students think about them, designing a teacher evaluation form for the purpose will be an interesting challenge for a staff committee. Initially, such a survey should only be for informational purposes, not part of your evaluation. Each teacher should be able to keep the responses confidential. *Such a program should only become part of the evaluation process if the teacher(s) agree(s) to it.*

There are things you can observe in children's behavior that can shed light on their attitudes toward the teacher. When students feel positive about a teacher, they will:

- Smile at the teacher.
- Talk to the teacher during free time, or on the playground.
- Joke and tease the teacher, in appropriate ways.
- Share details of their life outside of school.
- Show the teacher a prized object or project.
- Comment favorably about the teacher in her presence, or when talking with others.
- Have physical contact with the teacher in appropriate ways.

1.13   Using Information from Parents in the Evaluation of Teachers

Too often the administrator will hear about a teacher from parents only when they are dissatisfied. When the administrator gets such reports, the teacher is usually informed of the negative evaluation. Many parents are aware that the administrator is the appropriate channel for grievances, but there are usually few formal procedures for eliciting praise from parents.

In order to use parents in the evaluation of teachers, *it is necessary to provide methods by which both positive and negative information can be ob-tained.*

In using parents' opinions, the administrator should handle them as indi-cators, not as part of a substantive evaluation. Negative comments from a few parents may be more an expression of a point of view than an evaluation of a teacher's performance.

As suggested in Section 1.123, regarding children, it is best to "pilot" a parent survey, having teachers involved in its design, with their consent. As teachers see that you are making efforts to elicit positive feedback as well as criticism, parent opinion can begin to be used in the evaluative process.

1.14   Using Evaluation to Improve Teacher Performance

As stated in the introduction to this chapter, we believe that the goal of evaluation is to improve performance. The following sections describe methods for doing so.

1.141   Using teacher self-evaluation

A useful discussion about an evaluation can result from seeking to identify discrepancies between the teacher's sense of her own performance, and the administrator's analysis of it. For such discrepancies to be illuminated, the teacher must be familiar with the criteria used in the evaluation, and do a self-assessment along the same parameters as that done by the administrator.

Doing a self-assessment insures that the teacher is integrally involved in the evaluation. The teacher's opinions about her own performance are definitely given weight in the final analysis. Having teachers take a hard look at themselves may ease some of the conflicts that may be associated with evaluation.

If a teacher is more critical of some aspects of her behavior than you are, it provides the opportunity for positive feedback and supportiveness. It allows you to help a teacher move toward higher goals, even though her performance is adequate.

If you and a teacher judge some aspects of her behavior similarly, it clarifies the perceptions you share. If both of you feel positive about some things, it eases the discussion by providing areas of agreement about things you're both com-fortable with. If both of you identify areas of weakness, the onus of "judgment" is removed, and a "problem-solving" approach can be taken. It is in areas in which you are more critical of the teacher's performance than the teacher is that conflict may arise. In using this approach, such areas become specific, and thus, more easily discussed.

Remember that the goal of dealing with discrepancies is to *narrow the discrepancy*. If this approach is taken, then it is not necessary for one of you to win or lose. You and the teacher may have different standards by which you are measuring some factor. Because of differing experiences, some dimensions such as control, warmth, etc., mean different things to each of you. The process of clarifying can modify both opinion *and* behavior, so that the area of disagreement narrows. It may provide new insight into the teacher's style.

1.142 Criteria for discussing evaluations

"Well, where do we start?" You are ready to begin discussing your observations with a teacher whom you are evaluating. You may be faced with the problem of how to talk about it. We will suggest several approaches that can focus the discussion.

• One has already been described in some detail in Section 1.141—that of focusing on the discrepancies between yours and the teacher's observations.

• Discussions may be based on the degree to which teachers are meeting objectives. This presupposes that there is a set of them that teachers are prepared to discuss.

• Another approach is to have the teacher identify areas of discomfort in her own performance, or things she is having a hard time accomplishing.

• It is useful to base the evaluation session on a teacher's needs. Assess with the teacher what she needs in order to do what she would like to.

• A case study approach gives you opportunity to point out areas of both strength and weakness to a teacher. Either you or she selects problem situations or conditions in her classroom or teaching. Selecting recent problems is helpful.

There are two important outcomes of an evaluation discussion:

a. The teacher should have a more balanced and realistic view of her performance.
b. The teacher should be confident about her performance, and hopeful that she will receive help in areas where her performance can improve.

If these two things happen, your relationship with teachers will take care of itself—you will be a valued resource and sympathetic leader.

Whatever criteria are used in discussing evaluations, the goal should be to identify areas of possible growth, and help the teacher develop the resources for growing in those areas. This implies that evaluation discussions have a *future* orientation. Both of you seek some goals or directions that are different from those you've had in the past, either to correct weaknesses, or to add to the teacher's competence.

1.143 Handling fears, defensiveness, and resistance

These issues are often so stressful for many administrators that they have been dealt with at greater length in other sections of the Handbook. See relevant sections in Chapter 4, "How to Resolve Conflicts," and Handling Stress, Section 8.6.

1.144 How to help a teacher change

Among the goals of an effective evaluation process are increasing the flexibility of teachers' behavior in the classroom, and reducing the degree to which the teacher is limited by ineffective habits. In order to do this, you must be able to suggest alternatives *that teachers are capable of performing*.

Rather than telling a teacher to *change* some behavior, it is a better approach to encourage her to *experiment* with alternative behaviors, in order that she may observe, for herself, the effects that different approaches have on children. If a teacher is excessively retiring and soft spoken, and is having control problems (not that all soft-spoken teachers do), then you might encourage her to self-consciously speak louder. By using this approach, you attempt to build a feedback mechanism into the teacher's efforts.

It is important to ask the teacher what kinds of assistance you can provide to the "experiment." Such things as observing her, talking with her after she tries an alternative, etc., may provide needed support.

The things that people do that are justified or explained as being reflections of one's personality, are tied closely with the beliefs a person has about himself, and are central to feelings of self-esteem. When suggesting alternatives, it is necessary to understand those beliefs, so that new behaviors can become part of that belief.

As an example, if a teacher believes (and says) it is important to be gentle and kind with children, providing affection and comfort—but you feel she needs to be more assertive in order to manage the class better—then it will be necessary to point out how assertive behaviors are also expressive of her values by protecting children from failure and punishment, making rules clear so that they understand, etc. Promoting change requires that new alternatives make sense within the belief system of the teacher.

1.145 Setting up goals and objectives for teacher performance

Goals and objectives for teacher performance that arise from evaluations should be distinguished from those of the school, district, or state. They are not program goals.

If, as an example, a teacher needs to improve the way in which she handles discipline problems in her classroom, it will be necessary to specify a list of things that she must do. Such a list may include new procedures, as well as new behaviors with which she can experiment.

The items on such a list need to be concrete; the teacher should understand what each involves; and she must know that the resources in materials, time, or assistance, will be available. The objectives defined through this process should be reached in a short time, or else teachers' commitment to them will wane, and old habits will reassert themselves.

See chapters on Goal-Setting and Planning for additional suggestions.

1.2   EVALUATING YOUR PERFORMANCE AS AN ADMINISTRATOR

Evaluation is a two-way street. Whether or not there is any formal method for your staff to evaluate you, their assessment of your performance will be reflected in their feelings about you, the way they relate to you, and the degree to which they take responsibility within the school.

If there is some way for them to tell you what they think of you, and through this, they can influence your administrative behavior, then it is likely that the staff will be both more sympathetic and responsive to your leadership.

1.21   How Evaluating the Administrator Can Improve the School's Program

There are a number of important benefits that can arise from having a periodic staff evaluation of the administrator.

• It provides a mechanism for feedback to you about the areas in which teachers' dissatisfaction exists.

• The process symbolizes your willingness to listen and respond to teachers' concerns.

• It will let you know the areas in which your performance is adequate and appreciated by teachers. Your own self-esteem requires such positive feedback, and it's important to know what areas of your performance are "working."

• Having information about staff attitudes can allow you to foresee areas of potential conflict.

• Your willingness to be evaluated by teachers, provides an example of openness and willingness to change.

• Such a process enhances the climate of openness within the school, reducing the negative effect of criticism and blame, rumor and gossip, and unstated dissatisfactions.

1.211 Examples of the positive effects of evaluating the administrator

Mar Monte School District was in a small mountain community, in which Hal Burnett was both superintendent and administrator of the elementary and middle schools. His superintendent duties involved a great deal of time, and he had little involvement with the staff of the elementary school. He had organized the school so that resource teachers assumed much administrative responsibility, and reported to him about problems in the school.

Although Hal had indicated to several teachers that he desired more direct feedback from them, the staff was reluctant to make demands on his time. Most of the staff did not have a personal relationship with him.

The Title I consultant had been conducting inservice sessions with the staff. These had been arranged by the Title I resource/coordinator. Dr. Pascal, the consultant, was frustrated by the staff's reluctance to venture into new areas because of their apprehension about Hal's reaction. Finally, Dr. Pascal broached the subject with the staff (Hal almost never had time to attend the inservice meeting). They admitted that their approach with Hal was to let sleeping dogs lie. They recognized that Hal was under pressure from the community (they supported his position); there were problems at Middle School; and Hal was effective at getting money for the special programs.

Dr. Pascal suggested that since they felt positive about a number of things Hal did, it might be appropriate to let him know what the staff *liked* about his performance. Perhaps by emphasizing his strong points, and encouraging him to do more along those lines, some of their criticisms could be resolved. This was discussed among them, and Hal was invited to the next inservice meeting.

During the meeting, one of the resource teachers gave the background of the issue, and told Hal that the staff knew he wanted feedback about his performance, and had come up with a number of items that they appreciated, and wished to see him more. Hal was both embarassed and delighted with the positive feedback (it occurred on the same day as a very conflictive Board meeting), and asked the staff for some critical comments also, which could be provided at another meeting. This was done.

As a function of the positive climate that was produced by these two sessions, Hal began to appear in classrooms more often, and the teachers felt that he was more approachable than he'd been in the past. The encouragement from staff pushed him into reorganizing his time.

Angelo Martucci was in his first year as administrator at Crumm Elementary School. Under his predecessor, teachers had little to say about the way decisions were made at the school. This resulted in a good deal of gossiping, bickering among the staff, cliques, and resentment.

Mr. Martucci sensed that these things were still going on, in spite of his efforts to involve staff in planning and goal setting. It was not going well.

After three months on the job, Martucci announced in a staff meeting that he would like feedback from the staff about how his ideas were affecting teachers. He stated that he knew that he did things differently than his predecessor did, and wanted to know how the staff felt about the changes.

He had constructed a questionnaire (see Section 1.22) which the staff members completed anonymously. During the week following, he analyzed the responses, and discovered that about one-third of the staff felt mistrustful about the changes, and still felt that they had no power. This minority of the staff, nevertheless, colored the views of the majority. One of the oustanding points was that many teachers still were unclear about Martucci's "philosophy," and were apprehensive about what he intended for the future.

Martucci had a feedback session during the next staff meeting, in which he pointed out both the positive and negative responses to the questionnaire, indicating the percentages of staff members who gave different responses.

He shared more of his goals for the school, acknowledged that some of the criticism of him was valid, but added that he needed more specific information from individuals about their concerns, so that he could resolve matters more effectively, and change what he could.

At the conclusion of the meeting, two teachers, who had been most distant with Martucci, approached him about speaking with him. They told him that this was new for them, and they really hadn't been sure about his motives. His candor during the meeting had convinced them of his sincerity, and they were willing to do their part to help out with the changes.

Over the next several weeks, teachers became more vocal in staff meeting, several task forces were set up to work on special problems, and the staff seemed more comfortable.

Belva Summers had been administrator at McClure Elementary for four years. She had served previously as administrator at two other schools. Mrs. Summers was no novice at school administration.

This year, though, had been one in which many changes had happened to her, both personally and professionally. During the previous summer, she had attended a month-long "Renewal Workshop" for school administrators. Meeting other administrators from across the country, and hearing from national experts in all aspects of school affairs, had impressed her deeply. It was the most forceful experience, professionally, that she had had in years. Upon returning to school, she had instituted some new features in staff organization, meetings, and record keeping. She was pleased with the results so far.

A personal tragedy had occurred in her life several months ago. She and her husband had decided to separate after a ten-year marriage, and were in the process of divorcing. Being a professional, Mrs. Summers had let several teachers with whom she was friends know about her situation, but had attempted to isolate her personal life from her work at school.

In addition to these things, central office had made some new requirements of the building administrators. Mrs. Summers was somewhat unsure of the impact her changing duties were having on the staff.

All in all, Mrs. Summers was aware that to the members of her staff she must appear to have changed quite a bit. This became apparent when several of them began to tease her in staff meetings, by saying things like, "What now, Belva?", and "Here we go again, tell me what to do now!" When her closest friend on the staff said, jokingly, "Belva, why don't you take a vacation, so we can have one?", Mrs. Summers became aware that a subtle change had occurred in the relationship between her and a number of teachers.

Reviewing her notes from the summer workshop, she came across some material on self-evaluation for administrators, and decided to use it to get feedback from staff about herself. There was some precedent for this, since she had asked staff to evaluate her several years previously.

She announced in staff meeting that she was aware that many changes had occurred during the year in school, and in her own ideas (she still avoided bringing up the divorce), and she felt the need for some feedback from staff at this time. She wanted to know not only how they felt about things, but also any observations that they had about new directions for the school.

There were several interesting results of the survey, which she analyzed after the staff had completed the questionnaire. Almost all of the staff put their names on their responses, although she had told them they could be anonymous. She knew that this implied a good deal of trust on their part. A large number of staff members (there were 40 certificated members on the staff), reported that the clarity of communications was not to their satisfaction. Most of the staff felt that the goals of the school had changed, but were not sure of the reasons for it. Many staff members indicated that Mrs. Summers was not available for discussions about problems they were having.

In a space left for comments, about 20 percent of the staff voiced concern that they had perceived her as being more harried and "up-tight" than she had been before. Several said, "Relax!"

Mrs. Summers was affected by the general tone of personal concern that came through the responses. She also was not aware that she had changed so much in areas pointed out on the survey.

After reviewing the survey, she invited several of her friends from the staff to her home one evening, and asked them to review the results with her. They were quite candid in supporting the staff's views.

In her feedback session to the staff, Mrs. Summers was open with them about her reactions, and asked if there were some who would be willing to serve on teams to review the problem areas with her, and make sure that appropriate communications occurred before any future changes. Several teachers volunteered, and with staff participation and open communication, the climate gradually improved.

1.212   Building responsibility in staff, and reciprocity in behavior

Power means having the ability to influence the circumstances that affect one's life. Just as your evaluations will affect staff behavior, so will staff evaluation of you influence what you do. This sense of mutual influence will, if properly handled, increase awareness of reciprocal responsibility. The only way to build a sense of *responsibility* is to insure that a sense of *responsiveness* is built into the system.

When a staff of a school sees that it can collectively influence the way things happen at the school in concert with (not in opposition to) administration, that staff will feel more commitment to, and responsibility for, the program and procedures in that school.

If you will refer to Chapter 6, "Developing Greater Self-Esteem," and read the section on power, you will understand how staff evaluation of your performance can have a positive effect on the school.

1.22   How Staff Can Measure the Performance of the Administrator

We would like to suggest some guidelines for conducting a survey of staff opinions. See Figure 1-1.

DO	DON'T
1. Create items for a survey that break down your job into specific functions.	1. Avoid asking for global judgments, such as, "Are you satisfied with the way I do my job?"
2. Provide a paper and pencil instrument, which allows staff to be anonymous if they wish, in order to increase candor.	2. Avoid beginning this process with an evaluation discussion. It is likely to engender confusion and anxiety, and elicit comments from only a portion of the staff.

FIGURE 1-1

3. Have enough items on the survey so that strong *and* weak points can be evaluated.	3. Avoid only seeking criticism about your performance. It provides a lopsided picture, and people will hold back criticism if they can't praise also.
4. Have a form that can be easily completed, and easily coded.	4. Open-ended, essay-type questions are difficult to complete, and very difficult to analyze objectively.
5. Provide feedback about the results as soon as possible. Give a complete picture of the responses.	5. Don't keep the information private. Staff need to know that you have heard them, and are taking it seriously.
6. Use the survey report as the basis of a follow-up discussion.	6. Avoid discussing things that are not on the survey.

FIGURE 1-1 (continued)

1.221   Need satisfaction as criteria for evaluation

Teachers will have a positive attitude toward their administrator if they see him or her providing resources needed to do their job. This is the main relevance you have to teachers. Therefore, it follows that staff evaluation of you is based on the degree to which they see you as satisfying their needs.

When staff are unhappy with their administrator, it is a result of two factors:

- The administrator is not providing something that is within his power to.
- The staff expects the administrator to do things that are not possible.

Finding out what staff believe they need, and assessing the extent to which they see you as being responsible for satisfying those needs, begins the process of sorting out these two issues. *Not all expectations of all staff members are reasonable.* Knowing the proportion of dissatisfaction in your staff can help you keep things in perspective.

Growth in your job involves increasing your capability to meet the needs of staff. At any point in time, this involves an assessment of their needs and what you can or can't do about them. Surveying their needs can give you such information.

In the following section, we will delineate areas in which your staff may look to you for the satisfaction of their needs.

1.222   What staff needs from you as an administrator

Staff members need more from you than having adequate supplies of paper in the store room. Any area in which there is considerable dissatisfaction, can undermine staff's feelings about you in other areas.

Based on their needs, staff will evaluate your performance in the following areas:

a. How well you provide material resources necessary to their work.
b. Whether you are supportive in their dealings with parents.
c. How clearly you make known policies, rules, and regulations.
d. How well you manage meetings.
e. Whether you back them up in disciplining children.
f. Whether you provide leadership in designing educational goals.
g. How effective you are in facilitating problem solving.
h. Whether you make decisions effectively.
i. How much you listen to their concerns, and integrate them into your performance.
j. Whether you make them feel that they are important to the success of the program.
k. Whether you have good interpersonal relationships with them.
l. How well you handle administrative functions.

1.223   Items you can use on a staff survey of your performance

We will now suggest items that you can use on a survey instrument that makes the above issues concrete and specific. There are a number of ways you can ask questions or compose statements that illuminate staff attitudes, but staff responses will basically fall into two categories:

1. The degree of satisfaction they experience from that behavior.

   Satisfied ....Dissatisfied

2. The frequency with which they perceive you performing that behavior.

   Always ....Never

Note: When designing response categories, use an even number of them. This will prevent people scoring the average, and shows the trend more clearly. As examples:

1	2	3	4		
Always	Frequently	Sometimes	Never		

1	2	3	4	5	6
Very Satisfied	Often Satisfied	Somewhat Satisfied	Somewhat Dissatisfied	Often Dissatisfied	Very Dissatisfied

Now let's look at staff needs as applied to your performance. Refer to the items listed in Section 1.222.

a. Material resources.
   1. Provides supplies and materials in sufficient quantities.
   2. Clarifies supply budget, and orders what staff needs.

     3. Makes it hard to find materials I need.

     4. Provides materials and information when I need them.

b. Supportiveness with parents.

     1. Backs me up in conflicts with parents.

     2. Supports staff in parent relations.

     3. Helps staff understand attitudes of parents, and vice versa.

     4. Tries to stay out of conflicts between teachers and parents.

c. Clarifies policies and rules.

     1. Makes school policies clear.

     2. Insures that I understand the rules and regulations.

     3. Makes clear to staff what they can and can't do.

     4. Is confused about school policies and regulations.

d. Meetings.

     1. Conducts meetings well.

     2. Insures that meetings are clear and relevant.

     3. Is disorganized in conducting meetings.

     4. Meetings are productive and interesting.

e. Discipline.

     1. Helps clarify discipline procedures to children.

     2. Supports me in disciplining children.

     3. Helps staff in upholding discipline of children.

     4. Interferes with staff in disciplining children.

f. Educational leadership.

     1. Helps teachers improve their educational practice.

     2. Clarifies goals of the program, and helps staff move toward them.

     3. Lacks leadership qualities.

     4. Is an educational leader.

g. Problem solving.

     1. Contributes to problems the school has rather than eliminating them.

     2. Helps teachers solve problems.

     3. Brings issues to staff's attention and proposes solutions.

     4. Is available when teachers have problems.

h. Decisions.

     1. Can be depended on to make good decisions.

     2. Avoids making decisions.

     3. Involves staff in decision making.

     4. Is decisive and clear in resolving problems.

i. Listens to teachers.

     1. Can go to him when I have a problem.

     2. Listens to staff concerns and responds appropriately.

     3. Takes the feelings and opinions of the staff into consideration.

     4. Is hard to reach when I have a problem or concern.

j. Makes staff feel important.

     1. Gives teacher the feeling that their work is important.

2. Treats staff as if they are professional equals.
3. Makes staff feel that they are unimportant.
4. Helps staff feel that they are valuable to the school.
k. Interpersonal relationships.
   1. Is distant and reserved with staff.
   2. Has warm personal relations with me.
   3. Is pleasant to work with.
   4. Has good relations with teachers.
l. Administrative functions.
   1. Is organized, and aware of things going on in school.
   2. Is disorganized and creates administrative problems.
   3. Handles his administrative duties well.
   4. Doesn't burden staff with excessive administrative demands.

1.224   Setting up an administrator evaluation team

In Section 1.11, we suggested creating a team or task force to work with you to clarify evaluation procedures for staff. An added function for such a group could be to assist in designing the evaluation for the administrator. This responsibility might result in an annual or semiannual evaluation.

Such a group can work with you as a support team to work out ways to deal with staff dissatisfactions. It might also assist you in clarifying to staff the limits and constraints imposed on you in your role as administrator.

If such functions were combined in one task force in your school you would have the beginning of an internal evaluation system. Such a group could move toward engaging staff with yourself in being responsible for the overall educational program of the school.

1.23   How to Give Feedback and Use the Evaluations to Improve Performance

Once you have information from your staff, it's important that they know that you have heard and understood them, and that you intend to take action.

1.231   How to let staff know what they collectively think about the administrator

If you follow the suggestions for designing a survey for staff to use in evaluating your performance, you will be able to count responses and give a numerical report to the staff about how they perceive you. This is a useful first step in presenting the results to them.

Depending on the number of issues or items in the survey, this could be a good deal of information, which might be overwhelming to some. It is, therefore, helpful to select two or three major themes or trends—those which seem to have the most significance—to highlight in the report.

It is important that you also convey your reactions to the evaluation. After all, it is about you! Giving a dry, statistical analysis, without your own personal response, will seem awkward and incomplete. Indicate the areas in which you perceive staff to be satisfied, as well as any criticisms that are uncovered. You may have some ideas for changes in some areas, which it is important to convey. Avoid giving ''yes, but'' responses, which are designed to justify or excuse your behavior. You may have cogent reasons for doing what you do, but the most important factor is that staff feel that you are hearing what they have to say, and not just explaining away their critique. It is better to say, ''I don't yet know what to do with this piece of information, but will have to think about it,'' than to criticize the criticism. Remember to acknowledge any positive evaluations.

The results of some parts of the survey may be ambiguous, e.g., the staff may be evenly divided in the way they evaluate something you do. In your report to them, you may ask for clarification—more detail or examples of what staff means. Attempt to understand (and have staff understand) why different segments of the staff may see you differently. No questionnaire can give you all the information that you need.

You can't please everyone all the time! It is therefore especially critical that your staff be aware that there is a range in the way your behavior is evaluated by them.

1.232   Identifying strengths and weaknesses in the administrator's performance

What may be seen as a weakness by some people may be seen as a strength by others. When analyzing the staff's evaluation of you, keep in mind that how staff judge you is a function of how they see you act. This means that the context or situation, the people involved, and the issues under consideration will influence how different people react to you. Your personality may not be the issue.

Some people may think that you listen to them; others may feel that you don't. Some may see you as being a strong leader; others may see you as an insensitive autocrat. All of this supports the need for seeking cases and examples in areas in which there is a significant degree of dissatisfaction. Each staff member needs to know that his or her opinion of you is only one view. Your feedback to staff should take their diversity into consideration.

It is also necessary to point out that in meeting the needs of some teachers, the needs of others are not met. Some may feel comfortable with meetings; others may find meetings boring and time consuming. Some teachers may look to you for aggressive leadership; others may wish to be free to "do their own thing."

Clarifying the various conditions that influence your behavior will help staff to understand the pressures under which you work. This places responsibility on individuals to let you know what their needs are, rather than assuming that you know what everyone needs.

1.233   Setting goals for administrative performance

As a result of evaluation, you can propose to the staff a set of goals or objectives for your own performance. This will allow the staff to know what things *you* are working on to improve the overall climate of the school and encourage a sense of common purpose between you and the staff.

Such goals or objectives should be as specific and concrete as possible. You may also wish to tell staff that you will report to them from time to time about your progress.

Such goals need to be coordinated with the functions defined for your job by district policy, and fitted in with your school's goals. (See chapters on Goal Setting and Reducing Stress.)

1.3   EVALUATING THE SCHOOL CLIMATE

In recent years, studies of work environments have produced criteria for evaluating organizations—the way people feel about them, the degree to which they promote productivity, and their strengths and weaknesses as humane institutions. In this section, we will describe ways to use the results of such research to analyze the climate of your school.

1.31   What is School Climate—Really?

"School climate" can mean different things to different people. This section will make the idea more concrete. Additional material on this topic will be found in Chapter 5.

1.311   Indicators of a poor school climate

School climate can be a vague and ambiguous quality. Every school has both positive and negative features—things done well and others done poorly. At what point can it be said that the *climate* of a school is poor? The following factors are indicators that something is amiss in a school. If several of these are present, at a level that makes people uncomfortable, it is a sign that a major problem exists in the way people feel about the school.

- An excessive degree of vandalism, which can be traced to the children who attend the school.
- Children's commitment to honoring rules and standards is minimal.
- Excessive conflict or negative feelings among the teaching staff, resulting in cliques and subgroups.
- Teachers complain about others to the administrator.
- Staff meetings are not held regularly, and they are characterized by excessive strife or disinterest.
- Teachers wish to transfer out of the school, and few teachers wish to transfer into it.
- Poor communication between administration and staff.
- Conflict between parents and school, in which neither group is comfortable with the perceived attitude or behavior of the other.
- Teachers lack enthusiasm or are lethargic about the possibility of new programs being adopted.
- A reluctance to change procedures or policies in the face of continued problems.
- Repeated complaints about materials and supplies being inadequate.
- Many discipline problems in the school.
- Teachers send an excessive number of children to the office for disciplining.
- One or a few teachers are dominant, with others being intimidated by them.
- Administrator feels tense or uncomfortable when with teachers, and a feeling of distance between the administrator and staff exists.

1.312   The factors involved in school climate that can be measured

There are published surveys and questionnaires that assess various aspects of the school's organization. These will be reviewed below. Before considering specific methods for measuring climate, it is important to understand what is to be measured.

Measuring school climate is *not* a way to judge whether you have a "good" or "bad" school. It should not be used for that purpose, nor should it be presented to teachers, parents, or administrators in that light. *Evaluating school climate is for the purpose of identifying areas in which conflict, stress, or dissatisfaction contribute to negative attitudes about the school, among personnel in the school, and about commitment to the school's purposes.*

There are two general areas in which attitudes about the school will fall. These are:

a. Those things which primarily have to do with interpersonal relations among the people in the school—including, friendship, trust, warmth, affection, and respect.

b. Those things which primarily have to do with the work orientation of the school—including clarity of rules and procedures, communications, effective organization, and availabilities of resources. (See Section 5.23 for material that illuminates this.)

Factors that measure the interpersonal climate of the school:

- How close people feel toward each other.
- How concerned and committed to their jobs people are.
- Whether people feel supported by each other and the administration.
- How friendly people are to each other.
- Whether people see themselves as growing professionally and personally in the school.
- Whether people feel respected and valued for their contributions.
- How free people feel to make their own decisions.

Factors that measure the work orientation of the school:

- Whether people see the school as having good planning and problem-solving methods.
- Whether the work demands of the school are too high.
- How the administration controls or influences people's behavior.
- Whether the environment is conducive to change and innovation.
- How clearly rules, policies, and procedures are communicated.
- Whether people see the school meeting its goals.
- Whether necessary resources are available.

1.32   Tools to evaluate school climate

In this section, we will describe survey instruments that can be used in evaluating the climate of your school. They can be used for a formal analysis of the school (which will involve coding and some minor statistical procedures), or can simply give you ideas for designing a more informal survey of your own.

The Work Environment Scale and the Organizational Climate Description Questionnaire have been used in many settings, and validation data is available for them. You may not need to be so scientifically rigorous in order to derive useful information about your school.

1.321   The Work Environment Scale[1]

The Work Environment Scale has been used to evaluate the social climate of many types of work units. The authors of this Handbook have used it effectively in various school settings. The wording of items can be altered to

---

[1]For more detailed information on the Work Environment Scale, write to Consulting Psychologist Press, Inc., 577 College Ave., Palo Alto, California 94306, or Dr. Rudolf Moos, Social Ecology Laboratory, Stanford University, Palo Alto, California 94306. Reproduced by special permission from ''The Work Environment Scale'' by Rudolf H. Moos, Ph.D., and Paul M. Insel, Ph.D. Copyright 1974. Published by Consulting Psychologists Press Inc.

apply to schools without decreasing the usefulness of the scale. Permission from the publishers is required for this.

The complete scale (Form R) has 90 items (there is a short-form available). We will describe the main subscales and give examples of some items. All items are scored as true or false.

1. Involvement: Measures the extent to which workers are concerned and committed to their jobs; includes items designed to reflect enthusiasm and constructive activity.
    11. There's not much group spirit around here.
    51. Few people ever volunteer.
    61. It is quite a lively place.
2. Peer cohesion: Measures the extent to which workers are friendly and supportive of each other.
    12. The atmosphere is somewhat impersonal.
    22. People take a personal interest in each other.
    72. Employees often talk to each other about their personal problems.
3. Staff support: Measures the extent to which management is supportive of workers, and encourages workers to be supportive of each other.
    13. Supervisors usually compliment an employee who does something well.
    33. Supervisors usually give full credit to ideas contributed by employees.
    43. Supervisors often criticize employees over minor things.
4. Autonomy: Assesses the extent to which workers are encouraged to be self-sufficient and to make their own decisions. Includes items related to personal development and growth.
    14. Employees have a great deal of freedom to do as they like.
    44. Supervisors encourage employees to rely on themselves when a problem arises.
    84. Supervisors meet with employees regularly to discuss their future work goals.
5. Task orientation: Assesses the extent to which the climate emphasizes good planning and efficiency, and encourages workers to "get the job done."
    5. People pay a lot of attention to getting work done.
    15. There's a lot of time wasted because of inefficiencies.
    35. This is a highly efficient, work-oriented place.
6. Work pressure: Measures the extent to which the press of work dominates the job milieu.
    46. There is no time pressure.
    56. It is very hard to keep up with your work load.
    76. There are always deadlines to be met.
7. Clarity: Measures the extent to which workers know what to expect in their daily routines and how explicitly rules and policies are communicated.
    27. Rules and regulations are somewhat vague and ambiguous.
    57. Employees are often confused about exactly what they are supposed to do.
    77. Rules and policies are constantly changing.

8. Control: Measures the extent to which management uses rules and pressures to keep workers under control.
   8. There's a strict emphasis here on following policies and regulations.
   18. People can wear wild-looking clothing while on the job if they want.
   68. Superiors do not often give in to employee pressure.
9. Innovation: Measures the extent to which variety, change, and new approaches are emphasized in the work environment.
   9. Doing things in a different way is valued.
   49. The same methods have been used for quite a long time.
   59. New approaches to things are rarely tried.
10. Physical comfort: Assesses the extent to which the physical surroundings contribute to a pleasant work environment.
    10. It sometimes gets too hot.
    30. Work space is awfully crowded.
    40. This place has a stylish and modern appearance.

The Work Environment Scale can give a comprehensive picture of the attitudes of the staff in your school. Details of cost, scoring, norms, and other data regarding its use must be obtained from the publisher (referred to above).

Some ways it can be used include:

• Have staff complete it two ways. The first is to answer the statements according to the way they *actually* see the school. The second is to answer as they *ideally* wish the school to be. The discrepancies between the two indicate the degree of dissatisfaction that staff experiences. Large discrepancies are usually indicative of problem areas.

• Use individual subscales to illuminate particular aspects of the school's climate.

• Add items that are of special relevance in your school. You will not be able to use validation norms to assess the results, but can, nevertheless, get important information about your school.

• Use the scale at two or more times during the year, in order to assess changes in staff attitudes.

• Compare your (and other administrators') scores with the staff average to see whether administrators and staff see the school similarly.

• In larger schools, compare average scores of different subgroups within the school.

1.322   The Organizational Climate Description Questionnaire[2]

This questionnaire has been widely used in research in school climate and organization, It consists of eight subtests, four of which describe aspects of

---

[2]*The Organizational Climate of Schools*, Halpin, A. W., and Croft, D. B. The University of Chicago, 1963.

teachers' behavior, and four of which describe the administrator's behavior as perceived by the teachers. This survey places greater emphasis on the influence of administrative leadership on school climate than does the W.E.S.

The subtests on teachers' behavior include:

1. *Disengagement* refers to teachers' tendencies not to be involved in those things that serve to help get the work of the school done.
2. *Hindrance* refers to the teachers' feelings that administration interferes with their work by imposing non-essential tasks.
3. *Esprit* refers to the morale of the staff, especially whether they feel their social needs are being met at work.
4. *Intimacy* refers to whether teachers have friendly social relations with each other, not related to work.

The subtests on administrators' behavior include:

5. *Aloofness* refers to the degree to which the administrator deals impersonally with staff, and maintains distance from them.
6. *Production emphasis* refers to how directive the administrator is regarding work of the staff.
7. *Thrust* refers to how the administrator tries to make things happen through his own personal efforts.
8. *Consideration* refers to the degree to which the administrator treats teachers in a humane way.

The items (64) on the O.C.D.Q. give a picture of staff/administration relationships—the focal point for determining the quality of the school climate.

1.323 Diagnosing Professional Climate of Schools[3]

This very useful book contains a compendium of survey instruments that can be used to assess various aspects of the organizational climate of schools. The material is divided into sections, which include problem solving, staff responsibilities, behavior, and resources, community involvement, and a useful section on diagnosing your school. Thirty individual survey questionnaires are included, which can be used to evaluate particular aspects of staff, administrative, and all-school functions.

1.33 Setting Goals for Improving School Climate

Having data about how people perceive the organization and climate of the school allows you and your staff to objectify which conditions in the school need

[3]*Diagnosing Professional Climate of Schools*, Fox, R.S. Schmuck, et. al. NTL Learning Resources Corp., Inc., 2817-N Dow Ave., Fairfax, Virginia 22030, 1973.

to be changed. The process for doing so is no different from the procedures described in Chapter 3, on Planning.

The virtue of submitting your school to an evaluation of its climate is that it helps you to specify what needs to change, rather than having dissatisfaction remain vague and amorphous.

Changing the climate of a school may involve altering *your* behavior, the way the members of the *staff* act, or the *organizational procedures* of your school. Sometimes all three areas need to be affected. What to change, how to change it, what to do instead of what you're presently doing—the answers to these depend on knowing what people think and feel. Evaluating your school's climate provides the information you need.

2

Problem - Solving Procedures
for the Administrator

Problems challenge us and expand our abilities; problems are essential for our growth as people and groups, as we enhance our knowledge of how to deal with them effectively. When we have to face the same problem over and over again because we are not enhancing that knowledge, frustration mounts.

We all have our favorite way to "solve" problems:

—"Be logical, calm, and don't let feelings interfere."
—"Might makes right."
—"Let's ignore it and hope it goes away."
—"This is not *our* problem."

Another way, a *problem-solving process*, will be examined in detail. The process has these steps:

1. Identify the problem.
2. Analyze the problem.
3. Generate multiple solutions.
4. Plan for action.
5. Foresee consequences of intended actions.
6. Take action.
7. Evaluate action.

Before examining the steps, it is necessary to look at the blocks to successfully performing problem solving.

2.1   CHARACTERISTIC BLOCKS TO GROUP PROBLEM SOLVING

The following blocks can occur at any time and can disrupt the process:

2.11   The Group Has Not Agreed on How to Reach Agreement

A group needs to agree on the behaviors that will facilitate the meeting (norms), and how decisions are to be made. They should focus on the following areas:

1. Chairperson's and recorder's roles.
2. Meeting times and promptness.
3. Helpful communication behaviors.
4. How to handle negative feelings.
5. How to evaluate meeting effectiveness (see Section 9.4 on meeting effectiveness).

The group needs to decide how they will make decisions. The possibilities are:

• By AUTHORITARIAN FIAT: The person with the most authority makes the decision and others agree. This is effective when a crisis requires that decisions be made quickly. Expect resistance if this is used often.

• By VOTE: The majority decides. It is useful when time presses and the total commitment and involvement of participants is not needed. Expect the minority to withold giving full energy to the project.

• By CONSENSUS: The group arrives at a decision with which all can live. This method does not require unanimity of viewpoint; people can differ in their views but agree to commit themselves to the decision that is made.

For consensus to work requires everyone to share honestly and not to give in just to placate. People need to provide logical reasons to justify their points, which requires them to separate their sense of importance from whether their ideas are accepted or rejected. This method takes longer than the other two tactics, and involves a higher level of communication skill. Consensus, when used correctly, makes maximum use of the staff's knowledge and resources, and increases commitment to decisions. The quality of solutions is higher than in the other methods.

For a staff to make the most efficient use of time and the best decisions, all three methods should be used depending on the situation.

2.12 Seeking Solutions Before Understanding the Problem

Have you ever voiced a problem in a staff meeting and received a flood of solutions? Many of them probably reflected the biases of the speaker and were unrelated to the problem you proposed. The danger in proposing solutions too early in the problem-solving process is that group discord will increase. Unless people agree on what the problem is, each will propose solutions to different problems.

2.13 Group Processes Used Are Inappropriate

(See chapters on communication, role clarity, effective meetings, and conflict resolution.)

Effective problem solving requires knowledge of the problem-solving process and the use of appropriate group procedures. Figure 2-1 describes the most common mistakes, and appropriate group processes:

INAPPROPRIATE PROCESS	APPROPRIATE PROCESS
1. Problem-solving discussions are held in groups of more than eight persons.	1. Use is made of small-group processes ("accordion method"). Discussions are held in groups of eight or less.
2. No agenda is prepared before meeting.	2. Agenda prepared before meeting through a method agreed upon by the group and distributed to participants.
3. Group meets without a designated chairperson and recorder.	3. Chairperson and recorder are selected by the group and have clearly defined functions.
4. People tend to use blaming, name-calling, insinuation, or silent, non-verbal expressions of dissatisfaction.	4. People use "I" messages and describe own feelings when expressing feelings. These statements are used to start a problem-solving process.
5. No attempt is made to systematically obtain feedback from members about the group's effectiveness and emotional tone.	5. Time is given to obtaining feedback during and after the meeting through open discussion and/or questionnaires.

FIGURE 2-1

2.14 Dealing with Cliques, Pressure Groups, and Alienated Staff

If there are pressure groups or resistant cliques that do not take part in the problem-solving process, there can be no effective solutions. You must involve these groups in the process. How can this be done?

1. Use a survey or questionnaire to define the extent to which staff are polarized or have divergent opinions (see Section 7.3 on questionnaires).

2. Emphasize that the school needs them to be part of the process. If people *choose* not to become a part, they will have to live with the solutions proposed by the rest.

3. Point out that you are not asking them to placate or agree to certain solutions; all need to agree to the *process* of problem solving.

2.15 Time Limitations

Most faculties that are under stress resist taking time to complete the problem-solving process. They try to arrive at solutions within too short a period, and move from crisis to crisis.

This can be dealt with by considering the following issues:

- Time *well* spent is usually not regretted. Clarifying objectives and having a plan will often encourage a staff to take the time.
- Specify the time that will be devoted to a task, and *stick to your own time constraints*.
- Understand that a "good" solution requires that tasks, responsibilities, time limits, and evaluation are all clearly specified. Your staff needs to do these things habitually. They can look back on effective planning.
- Point out to staff the man/hours saved by using committees instead of dealing with issues among the whole staff—e.g., if the whole staff discussed this for one hour, it would take 25 man-hours; if a committee of three discussed it for three hours, it would only take nine man-hours. Encourage the use of committees.

2.2 IDENTIFYING THE PROBLEM—THE FIRST STEP

Defining a problem is always somewhat arbitrary, as there are always interrelationships among many problems. But without some *agreed-upon* definition which focuses group discussion, there will be confusion.

A problem occurs when a discrepancy exists between a present condition and a hoped-for or desired state. A problem is "identified" when a group can agree on a stated definition of these two states. For example, see Figure 2.2.

PRESENT CONDITION	DESIRED CONDITION
• Frequent playground fights. • Children and staff confused about rules. • Staff complain about class-room discipline.	• Fights are infrequent. • Children and staff clear about rules and consequences. • Children follow school rules.

FIGURE 2-2

Note that a number of closely related aspects of the problem are stated. These are the primary indices of the problem.

2.21 Procedures for Identifying Problems

The following are some simple techniques which facilitate the process of problem identification.

2.211 Use questionnaires and surveys

Questionnaires and surveys can be used to narrow staff concerns to a manageable area. If there are dissatisfaction and conflicting opinions about what the problem is, you could profit from using a questionnaire.

1. Let staff know the purpose of the questionnaire and how results will be evaluated and fed back to them.

2. Consider a couple of formats:

A. Ask each person to list school problems (or any other broad areas), giving examples of the problem, and then rank order the problems according to their importance.

B. You list possible problems, leaving space for respondent to write in others, and then have the respondent rank order the list.

3. Feedback should be prompt and lead into problem-solving sessions, after selecting the high priority items.

2.212 To refine, use small group process

It is difficult and inefficient to hold discussions in groups larger than eight people. One method, called the "accordion method," can allow a large staff to hold discussions in small groups.

Case Example: The Bailey School Resource Center was chaotic. The resource teacher was threatening to quit and many teachers were not making use of the Center. The Center was located in the library and there was confusion about what was the Resource Center and what was the library.

The principal called a problem-solving meeting and divided the staff (randomly) into groups—four groups of six people. Each group had to agree within 20 minutes on a definition of the problem, stated in terms of "present state" and "desired state." Each group had a chairperson and recorder. In each group the members shared their statements of the problem, which were recorded on butcher paper. From these lists, through combining, restating, and discussion, a final statement of the problem was arrived at. When the total group was reconvened, these statements were placed on the blackboard for all to see. It became apparent that there were two distinct problems. One involved the lack of role clarity of the resource teacher; the other had to do with the space used, so that the library and Resource Center could serve their separate functions.

The statement of the resource teacher's problem was as follows:

PRESENT CONDITION	DESIRED CONDITION
Resource teacher frustrated and confused.	Resource teacher clear about role.
Staff have conflicting expectations of resource teacher.	Staff understand and are in agreement about resource teacher's role.
Teachers resistant to taking advice from resource teacher.	Resource teacher does not feel rebuffed by staff.

The problem of the use of space was as follows:

PRESENT CONDITION	DESIRED CONDITION
Resource material hard to locate.	Resource material varied and easy to locate.
Teachers feel more quiet is necessary when using library.	Library functions not in conflict with Resource Center purposes.
Resource Center feels cramped—use is limited.	Both functions grow in size and quality.

The staff was then sent back into their "accordion groups" to develop ideas about how to work with these two problems. All groups felt that both were related and critical problems, and the faculty divided itself to work on both simultaneously.

2.213   Use of feedback and multimedia

In the example of Bailey School, butcher paper and chalkboards were essential for feedback. The problem-solving steps were written down on a large sheet of paper and referred to throughout the subsequent sessions.

2.214   Refining the problem statement

The problem statement is only a starting point, a focus to channel energy and ideas, and is not fixed and immutable. New information about the problem which arises in subsequent sessions is added to the problem statement, which is placed in easy view of the group. It may be necessary from time to time to refer to the problem statement as a way of refocusing.

2.3   ANALYZING THE PROBLEM—THE SECOND STEP

It is essential that solutions be delayed until the problem can be analyzed. A way of doing this is through a method called "force field analysis."

2.31   Force Field Analysis

The procedure assumes that the present condition is the result of forces that facilitate movement toward a goal and those that hinder movement toward the ideal goal. See Figure 2-3.

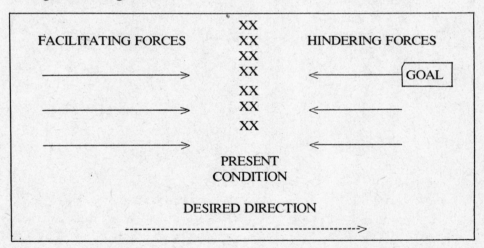

FIGURE 2-3

The procedure identifies the forces and selects the most important ones to work on. The steps are as follows:

1. Divide group into small subgroups of eight or less.
2. Divide a butcher paper sheet into two columns: one labeled "facilitating forces" and the other "hindering forces."

3. Each group brainstorms (freely lists without criticism) their ideas of what these forces are. The descriptions are listed on the butcher paper. Avoid long discussions of each item—just list what's said.

Make certain that each group considers "personal" as well as "situational" factors:

PERSONAL FACTORS are those that are characteristic of individuals—their fears, skills, motivations, biases, etc.

SITUATIONAL FACTORS include such things as space, money, materials, numbers of people, past history which has fostered group norms, policies, etc.

Realize that some factors have both facilitating and hindering aspects to them, e.g., new government programs, staff increases, etc.

4. The group now selects the three or four *most important and solvable hindering forces*. It is more effective to reduce the hindering forces than to increase the facilitating forces. The next step will use these selected forces as the basis for brainstorming solutions.

2.32   Example of Force Field Analysis for a Group

The faculty that developed its problem statement in Section 2.212 about the resource teacher used a force field analysis of the problem. They came up with the following list of hindering and facilitating forces:

FACILITATING FORCES	HINDERING FORCES
Staff likes resource teacher.	*Staff confused about resource teacher's expectations.
Resource teacher skilled and has ideas.	Confusion between resource teacher and staff on how best to give and receive advice.
Staff desires to improve reading and math performance.	*Resource teacher confused about expectations.
Parents interested in Resource Center.	Space not adequate for Resource Center.
District provides local school with Resource Center's budget.	Increase of staff at school has confused all roles.
	Time pressure makes it difficult for teachers to meet with resource teacher.
	*General discipline problems increase resistance to sending children to Center.

The staff working on this problem then selected the most important and solvable hindering forces as indicated by asterisks above.

2.33 How to Do the Force Field Analysis Alone

You can use the force field analysis in working on problems by yourself. The following suggestions will help you:

1. Try not to complete the process in one sitting.

2. Talk with a friend about the analysis and have this friend help you in defining the most important and solvable hindering forces.

3. Give yourself a fixed time for brainstorming ideas, a period where you hold back criticizing your ideas.

For example, Bill Martin, principal of Freemont Elementary School, often went home after school feeling exhausted and worried. He was willing to feel tired from working hard, but not exhausted and tense. One evening he decided to take a closer look at the factors that were affecting him. He brainstormed for ten minutes and then let the ideas rest for a couple of days before returning to them. He had thought of a couple of new ideas during this time. At school, Bill also talked to a friend, the school psychologist, who helped him clarify his list.

After distilling a long list of both facilitating and hindering forces, Bill selected a few of the hindering forces for more intense scrutiny. These included:

a. I'm a new principal, and feel that I lack organizational skills.
b. I'm afraid to lay it on the line to staff members who seek my advice— afraid to hurt their feelings.
c. Too many new programs confuse staff roles.

2.34 Additional Points to Remember in Doing Force Field Analysis

1. In deciding whether a hindering force is solvable, you need to look at staff and school resources such as available skills, motivation of staff, extent of problem, time, and money.

2. When doing group force field analysis, avoid making hindering forces "personality" issues. Although fears, biases, etc., are factors, try stating these as indicating a *relationship* in which both parties share the responsibility; e.g., instead of saying the resource teacher was a shy and timid person, it was stated that she was confused about staff expectations (see Chapter 4 on conflict resolution).

In personal use of force field procedure, your thoughts and fears can and need to be examined openly.

3. Staff needs to be complimented at the end of this step for defining the

problem and forces, without getting caught up in solutions. From now on solutions will be sought.

2.4   GENERATING MULTIPLE SOLUTIONS—THE THIRD STEP

Having more than one way to solve a problem increases the likelihood that *something* will work. The following material will show you how to go about doing so, without having chaos.

2.41   Brainstorming

The purpose of brainstorming is to produce many ideas in a short period of time; quantity rather than quality is important. The rapid release of ideas in a noncritical atmosphere in which people are encouraged to voice unusual solutions can lead to highly creative, yet practical solutions.

In order to set up the brainstorming procedure correctly, the rules need to be written and posted as follows:

1. The brainstorming period will last _____ minutes (usually 15 minutes).
2. Come up with as many ideas as possible—quantity rather than quality is the goal.
3. Hold back all criticism or praise of ideas.
4. Don't discuss ideas; this will occur later.
5. Come up with at least one "silly" idea in order to release other imaginative ideas.

Divide the staff into small groups of four to eight. Each group will brainstorm one of the hindering forces selected in the previous step. Write the "force" to be focused on at the top of a sheet of butcher paper, which the group will use to list their ideas. Have the group select a recorder.

2.42   Stimulating Group Creativity

1. You can facilitate brainstorming by reminding the group of the rules if they fail to follow them. Alert the groups that you will do this if necessary.

2. The facilitator should contribute some outlandish ideas so as to help establish a permissive atmosphere.

3. Warm up the group by asking each member to contribute a "crazy" idea. Write these ideas on the butcher paper. Another warm-up idea is to have a person give an idea which the person to his right has to extrapolate into a *more* "silly" suggestion.

4. Have the ideas written on the paper so that everyone in the small group can see them; often new ideas are generated by a review of the previous ones.

5. Regular use of brainstorming in faculty meetings (and in the classroom with children) will foster a norm for creative solution seeking.

2.43 Selecting the Best Solution

After brainstorming, you need to select the best solution in terms of:

1. FEASIBILITY: Do you have the time, money, and skills to do it?
2. RELEVANCE: Will the successful completion of the idea lead toward your goal?

The following steps will help the group to select the best idea:

1. Go over each item on the list; be sure that the idea is clearly understood. Cross out ideas that everyone feels are impractical, and check those which most people feel positive about.

2. Review those checked ideas to determine which would be most appropriate to start on. Other useful ideas should be held until later (see #3, below). Several ideas can be tried simultaneously if resources (time, money, skills) permit.

3. Write down on cards those ideas which were not selected in step #2, but still had merit (the ones that were not crossed out). These ideas may be useful later if circumstances change.

4. Develop support for the ideas by allowing interests to guide selection. For example:

—An artistic staff member wished to create posters.
—An ex-coach decided to develop a sports program to help with a group of unruly children.
—Three teachers who attended a self-esteem course at the local university agreed to set up time after school for three weeks to discuss classroom ideas for raising self-esteem in children.

5. Complex ideas may be a challenge that will stimulate the full range of staff talents. Survey staff interests to show how the implementation of the ideas fits their talents.

6. Point out how a particular solution will affect more than one problem. For example: clarifying rules and procedures as a way of meeting discipline needs will also help in establishing better communication between staff and administrator.

2.44 Case Examples of Creative Solutions to Common Problems

The following describes creative solutions that made a radical difference to the schools that acted on them.

1. A staff painted the doors of the school bright colors since the district did not have the money to improve the school aesthetically.

2. Teachers who needed more information about the quality of their program surveyed the fifth grade children about what they liked about the school and what problems they faced.

3. Children's alienation and disinterest were resolved in one school by the establishment of mini-courses which were determined by the children's interests and hobbies. The courses were held on Friday afternoons, and staffed by volunteers and teachers.

4. The problem of low staff morale was solved at one school by establishing a calendar that indicated staff members' birthdays. Something special (a birthday cake, little gift hidden in their closet) was done on that day. The school also started a "Secret Pal" system where staff members received written compliments and positive messages, but did not know who had sent them. At the end of the year, the name of the sender was revealed. Each person had previously drawn (at random) names of people to whom they would write.

2.5 PLANNING FOR ACTION—THE FOURTH STEP

The ideas that have been selected as workable now need to be developed into a *program*. The program will specify the activities that will bring the ideas to reality.

2.51 Planning Procedures

Planning procedures are detailed in Chapter 3. The plan should have four components:

1. Which activities are to be completed?
2. Place each activity in a logical time sequence.
3. Who will perform each activity?
4. What resources need to be obtained—such as money, released time, volunteers, consultants, central office decisions, etc.?

2.52   Clarifying Roles and Responsibilities

New ideas often imply new activities. Roles may need to be redefined. You must help staff through this redefinition.

Monitoring the plan is a function that requires roles to be clarified. It is helpful to form a steering committee consisting of staff members and the administrator, which has as its function the following duties:

1. Discuss the activities and allocate responsibilities for carrying out the day-to-day details of the plans.

2. Plan to deal with the problems that will emerge when new contingencies are faced.

3. Report to entire staff on progress and alert them as to the ongoing needs of the program.

There are several roles that need to be clarified under such a structure:

1. STEERING COMMITTEE CHAIRPERSON: (see Chapter 9 on effective meetings.) It is important to clarify the relationship of the chairperson to the administrator if the two roles are handled by different people.

2. ADMINISTRATOR: As administrator you may be involved in several steering committees. If there are several projects, you would thus:

—coordinate plans made by several committees
—clarify roles and policies
—help channel resources to the plan. One principal helped by taking over classes while teachers met with consultants.
—facilitate communication with the committee and between committee and rest of staff

3. COMMITTEE MEMBERS: The membership of the committee may be rotated among staff, but should involve those who are most interested in a particular plan. The committee needs to understand what decision-making powers they have been given and what feedback staff expects from them. If this is not done, you can expect staff resistance and a drop in involvement.

2.53   Keeping Records

Records are often troublesome to keep, but they are important.

1. They help in impressing people with the importance of following through on responsibilities.
2. They allow staff to build on previous ideas without wasteful backtracking.
3. They help evaluate progress and demonstrate effectiveness.

What kinds of records can do these important things?

1. Minutes of meetings that are clearly written and emphasize actions that were taken.
2. "Time line" charts (see Chapter 3 on planning) which are up to date, posted, and referred to when providing feedback to the staff.
3. A project scrapbook containing newspaper clippings, photocopies of activities, quotes of participants, children's drawings and reactions, etc. Such a document adds to the visibility of a program and helps maintain continuing interest.
4. Questionnaires and surveys that provide a base line by which progress can be measured.

2.6 STAYING OUT OF TROUBLE BY FORECASTING THE CONSEQUENCES OF INTENDED ACTIONS—THE FIFTH STEP

The best-laid plans often go awry. Taking stock of what's likely to happen if you do what you intend can provide insurance for success.

2.61 The Pause That Brings Success

It is often hard to take this pause. Staff will want to remain enthusiastic after discussing new ideas and may try to avoid "negative" thoughts. By this time, pressure will be mounting to "get on with it." You need to emphasize the importance of this step. Two things can be predicted:

1. The activities' impact on people in terms of time pressure, demand for skills, risk taking (how different are the activities from the routine?), arousing biases and prejudices, information needs, etc.
2. To what extent activities will provide movement toward the final goal.

How to Forecast

1. A good way to start is to divide staff into small groups; each group is to brainstorm possible consequences for a different group of people—parents, children, staff members on committee, staff, etc.
2. After the brainstorming, each group selects the most important consequences and reports back to the total group.
3. Any unacceptable consequences should guide modification of plans and will be used by the steering committee in monitoring programs.

2.62 Examples of Consequences

A district gave special leadership training to principals, including communication techniques. Teachers, however, saw principals use these techniques to manipulate staff and were suspicious of the special training. Only when staff were included in the training with their principal did resistance decrease.

At another school, the decision to try more innovative teaching involving individualized learning had a strong impact on the community, which was resistant to the ideas. At a meeting, the community attacked the consultant who was assisting the program, saying that he was experimenting with their children. The parents did not understand the desire of the faculty to be more creative in their teaching.

At a third school, faculty enthusiastically set up four plans centering on improving staff communication, innovative changes in classroom arrangement, increased parent involvement, and better school discipline. They had not been aware of the large amount of time that they had to devote to planning and carrying out these ideas. Two of the projects had to be dropped after three months, much to the disappointment of the staff.

All of the above consequences could have been avoided by taking time to anticipate the impact of the programs on the groups involved.

2.7   TAKING ACTION—THE SIXTH STEP

How you move ahead can be as much of a problem as deciding what to do. The following cautions need to be respected.

2.71   What One School Learned About Taking Action

Cherry Hill Elementary School decided to improve the children's human relationship skills. After several problem-solving sessions, the staff selected the following ideas:

1. Emphasize the student council, gradually giving the council more decision-making powers.
2. Increase use of the "magic circle," a program of small-group activities which improve relationship skills.
3. Start a "buddy system."
4. Hold a school festival involving parents.
5. Ask parents to reward a child when the teacher sends home notes describing the child's positive social behavior.
6. Use questionnaires measuring "caring" behaviors as a way to assess the program.

A steering committee was formed and asked the school psychologist to help develop the assessment instruments. They soon found that it took more time than anticipated to finish the questionnaire. Sam Jones, the principal, found that he had to attend a number of central office meetings. His absence presented a challenge to the committee chairperson to take more initiative; she hesitated, but finally did move ahead with the plans. The committee also interviewed several consultants offering role-playing training, and selected two for discussion with the staff.

At the next staff meeting, they approved the questionnaire and selected a consultant. It also emerged that many staff members were unsure about how to set up the buddy system. One of the experienced teachers held a training session one afternoon.

In implementing the plan during the year, the staff found out the following things:

1. Mr. Jones had to take a more active role in involving parents, which required him to be excused from some central office meetings.

2. Schedules had to be shifted to allow several teachers to visit exemplary student council meetings at other schools.

3. An unanticipated vocal contingent of parents attacked the "magic circle" activities as therapy. Staff decided to de-emphasize this until parents had a chance to be more involved in the program.

4. The steering committee found it had to remind the staff about how the activities contributed to the program's progress. This was particularly important in the middle of the year when staff attention shifted to the possibility of receiving state funds for an early childhood education program.

5. Mr. Jones found he had to work with several teachers who felt totally inadequate to use role playing, even after inservice training.

6. Finally, the program was a success. The questionnaires did show improvement. The staff decided to continue developing human relations skills for another year in order to solidify the gains.

2.72 Some Things to Remember When Taking Action

1. Unexpected events, new priorities from central office, unanticipated resistance will necessitate shifts in program. Such shifts need to be carefully communicated and indicated on the master plan.

2. You can drop an activity, but still keep the overall goal in mind.

3. Changes need to be decided on and not allowed to "just happen" without deliberation. Otherwise, people will feel a loss of power and ability to control the process.

4. Changing routines often brings stress. It may stem from feeling inadequate to perform new skills, not knowing what to expect, an increase in the need for information, and threats to "territorial" needs, such as having to "share" one's children or space with others.

2.73   How You Can Help People Accept Change

1. Make the program structure and direction clearly visible through charting activities completed and those yet to be done; make periodic reports to total staff and parents on the results of activities. Such a visible structure helps people feel more secure.

2. Involve as many people as possible in the decision making that is affecting their work. People *increase* their resistance to change when they *don't* have a voice in the change.

3. Create a climate for people to accept mistakes and misunderstandings as a normal part of change, and not as indicators of personality defects. Be able to admit your own mistakes.

4. Emphasize the positive aspects of the program and indicate awareness and appreciation for staff efforts.

5. Listen to frustrations and give time for them to be aired at meetings and in your office.

6. Indicate that shifts in activities are o.k., not a sign of personal inadequacy or program failure.

2.8   EVALUATING ACTION—THE SEVENTH STEP

Through proper evaluation we know if our actions are leading us to our goal. It is harmful and wasteful to continue a program that is not working. There are two types of evaluation that need to be performed:

1. Evaluation of program objectives (see Section 3.2 on objectives)— usually at the end of a program.

2. Ongoing assessment of the impact of activities on program participants. Such periodic assessments pick up information that may affect subsequent activities and thus the total impact of the program, e.g., staff and parent attitudes toward program changes.

2.81   Methods of Evaluation

There are several methods you can use to evaluate programs. Often a combination of them works best.

2.811   Surveys and questionnaires

The use of surveys and questionnaires has been discussed in a number of places (see Sections 1.223, 4.5, 7.31). These methods are relatively inexpensive and done quickly. They can be used—

- After parent meetings to obtain participants' reactions.
- To survey staff morale after forming new teaching teams.
- To assess staff observations about the impact of a new reading program on students.
- To gather information from students about classroom activities that were helpful in raising their self-esteem.
- To determine changes in staff attitudes toward individualized education after a minimum day workshop.

To develop your own questionnaire, form a work committee which can:

1. Brainstorm areas to be covered by the questionnaire.
2. Determine length of questionnaire and question format.
3. Write the questions.
4. Help in administration of the questionnaire.
5. Evaluate results and help in feedback.

The following are alternative question formats:

- *Sentence completion:* "It is difficult to carry out this activity when _____."
- *Open-ended questions:* "Describe the extent to which today's workshop met your expectations."
- *Multiple choice and rating:* "Rate between 0 (low) and 10 (high) the extent to which this workshop helped you to understand the Hays Reading Method."
- *Rank order items:* "From 1 (most helpful) to 5 (least helpful), rank the following school/community services in terms of which have been of the most help to you:"

_____ Film night
_____ Discussion of legal problems Tuesday evenings
_____ Raising self-esteem of children course
_____ Folk dancing
_____ Nutrition course

2.812 Records

Keeping records is a way of regularly counting and classifying events. Whenever possible, use routinely gathered records as a part of the evaluation, e.g., number of children going to the infirmary, number of incidents of school vandalism and cost of damage, number of days of staff absence, average number of parents attending community/school meetings.

Usually, special records need to be developed for projects, such as:

- Number of playground rule violations.
- Frequency profile of how many children checked out a given number of library books.
- Daily average of children sent to office for discipline.

Record keeping should involve as simple and objective recording of frequency of events as possible without extensive use of teacher time.

2.813 Interviews

Interviewing selected (maybe at random) participants in programs is often not possible unless funds are available to hire an experienced person. Interviewing is time consuming. Furthermore, information given by the interviewee is strongly affected by that person's relationship with the interviewer. An administrator is not in the best position to get objective information because of many people's reaction to his authority.

Nevertheless, interviewing can be used as a preliminary step to determine what should be explored more deeply in a questionnaire. It is important to select interviewees who are knowledgeable, feel comfortable with the interviewer, and can describe their observations and reactions.

2.82 Making Evaluations Part of the Planning Process

Evaluations take time, money and personnel and thus affect the resources available for a program. It is therefore important that evaluating procedures be built into the plans that emerge from the problem-solving process. Who will do what by when with what resources? People tend to underestimate the time needed to develop evaluation procedures and assess results of questionnaires. Time should be allocated for consultations with those who can assist in selecting and developing evaluation instruments.

2.83 Using Evaluation to Alter Direction

Evaluating program activities can uncover information that wasn't apparent in the planning stage, but is important enough to alter subsequent activities.

Case Example: Dunworth Elementary School, on the basis of a community need assessment which placed high priority on reading, had selected a new reading skills package. This package presented a detailed breakdown and sequential arrangement of the reading skills objectives toward which staff directed their teaching efforts. Central office and school board were impressed with the program and exerted pressure on the staff to accept it. Bob Berry noticed that staff had considerable difficulty in learning the objectives and scheduling time to do the testing required.

A staff meeting was held after several months to discuss the progress of the program. The district Director of Elementary Education was invited to attend. During the meeting, staff asked routine questions but they raised no serious issues. At the end of the meeting they completed an anonymous questionnaire about the meeting and reading program. Bob was shocked to discover that three-fourths of the staff indicated in their questionnaires strong objections to the time taken to follow the program and to the highly formal and constraining effect of the detailed objectives. When Bob asked a few teachers why these issues were not raised during the meeting, they indicated that the Director, a high pressure person, had a dampening influence. Bob also became aware of how his own enthusiasm for the reading program had cut off much needed communication between himself and many of the staff. Another meeting was called; the results of the survey were presented and solutions brainstormed. A committee was formed to look at alternative plans to the reading program, and a procedure was worked out by which teachers could develop their own reading objectives, but take into consideration the needs and objectives of the teachers in adjoining grades.

2.9 TEACHING PROBLEM SOLVING TO STAFF

It is essential that those using the problem-solving steps agree on and be familiar with the process. Figure 2-4 is an outline of a four-to-six-hour inservice program with a school staff. Details of this outline can be found in this chapter and related sections of this book.

I. INTRODUCTION
   A. What is a "Problem"
      1. Problems are to be expected, and they are not a sign of being "bad" or "weak."
      2. Problems are a discrepancy between actual conditions and ideal ones.
      3. Problems depend on individuals' viewpoints and perspectives.
   B. Blocks to problem solving
      1. Solutions before analysis.
      2. No agreement on group roles and behavior.
      3. Group processes inappropriate.
      4. Seeing the problem as an admission of weakness.
   C. Necessity for staff to agree on process
      1. Difference between process and content.
      2. Process not rigid and can be modified to suit staff situation.
   D. Briefly describe problem-solving steps
II. DEVELOPMENT OF GROUP NORMS
   A. Discuss importance of norms
      1. What are group norms?
      2. Why is it important to discuss and agree on norms?
         a. Certain behaviors hinder communication.
         b. Agreeing to discuss norms allows for a way of changing hindering behaviors.
         c. We control the process rather than the process controlling us.
      3. Discuss importance of agreeing to use small groups (accordion method) and the technique of "survey."
   B. Group discusses desired norms
      1. Group discusses "helping" and "hindering" behaviors; write these on board and get agreement.
      2 Group reaches agreement on behavior of chairperson and recorder.
      3. Group reaches agreement on when to use small-group process.
III. PRACTICE PROBLEM SOLVING STEPS
   A. Select a "practice problem"
      1. Avoid "crisis" problems because the strong feelings would interfere with becoming aware of the problem-solving steps process.
      2. Problem should be "real" and of concern to staff.
   B. Points to remember in leading group through steps:
      1. Describe step, including how participants need to behave at each step.
      2. After a step is finished, discuss the process; suggested questions:

        "How did you feel during this step?"
        "What did people do that helped?"
        "What did people do that hindered?"

IV. DISCUSS ENTIRE PROCESS AND REACH AGREEMENT ON HOW AND WHEN TO USE THESE STEPS IN SOLVING STAFF PROBLEMS

FIGURE 2-4

3

Planning – How to Set Goals and Reach Them

Participative management, decentralized decision making, democratic problem solving—all involve at least one common feature. That is the need for effective planning procedures that can be used in groups.

Effective management is based on good planning. This chapter shows how to work with your staff as a planning team.

3.1 GOAL SETTING

Planning is a way to prepare to take action toward a goal or purpose. Goals can either be implicit or explicit. When a number of people participate in planning, it is necessary that they agree on goals.

3.11 Goals as Statements of Long-Range, Comprehensive Purposes

Having commonly held, explicitly stated goals helps you and your staff to focus energies and have direction, and encourages cohesiveness within your school. Goals, which arise from the process that will be described in this chapter, establish common purposes for a staff.

When your staff has such common purposes, priorities about program activities become more self-evident, and the day-to-day things that have to be done become part of an overall pattern which has meaning.

You can save time and avoid conflict by clarifying the goals for your school.

3.12 Relationship to Feelings and Attitudes of Goal-Setting Group

When a group defines goals it gives substance to what people feel is important. People's feelings, attitudes, and expectations are critical to the success of achieving goals. They provide the energy and commitment that are necessary to do the work required to fulfill goals; motivation to action arises from feelings.

3.13 Goal Setting as an Opportunity for Visionary Thinking

The day-to-day tasks involved in teaching or managing a school often leave little time for thinking ahead to determine what it is that you and your staff want to accomplish. Things that seem to be impractical or unrealistic today may become real possibilities in the future. Goal setting can release the creative energies of your staff; effective planning can translate vision into realities.

In order for you to be an imaginative educational leader, you must have an opportunity to influence the thinking of your staff with your vision of what your school might do.

Your staff enthusiastically supports goals that reflect *their* visionary thinking. If goal setting does not tap into the hopes and desires of your staff, the end product will only be definitions of what you are already doing. Goals should move a whole system to a higher level of functioning.

One way to stimulate visionary thinking is as follows:

1. Prepare your staff for an exercise in visionary thinking, and have their permission and agreement to engage in a group exercise.

2. Ask the group to relax deeply. (See Section 8.3 on relaxation techniques.)

3. Pose the question, "What could be happening at our school one year from now, if really positive changes occur?"

4. Ask the group members to visualize very concrete events that could occur. They should be specific about what they foresee happening among children, teachers, parents, etc.

5. Have people list the images that they see individually, and then share them in small groups.

6. Have each small group list the images/ideas on butcher paper for displaying to all.

7. Identify the images that seem to be similar or in the same area. Pick out two or three major items for translation into goals.

3.14 Examples of Goal Statements

Some examples of goal statements might be:

- Children will seek out and enjoy an increasing number of opportunities for reading.
- Children will have a variety of alternatives for conflict resolution, and fighting will decrease.
- Staff members will engage in cooperative programs, mutual activities, and positive interaction with each other.
- Children will have a positive self-image.
- A significant number of parents will be involved in school activities.

3.15 Procedures for Helping Group Define Goals

Although many goals are implicit in the nature of a school's program, the selection of a few explicit, commonly held goals helps a staff focus energies, exercise creative behavior, and develop imaginative programs. Goals provide a challenge to see beyond the current demands, and identify a valued future state for the school.

3.151 Creating a future orientation

Once you and your staff agree to participate in a series of meetings in which school goals are to be clarified, you need to create a future-oriented climate within your staff. You can set the stage for this by posing the following question during the staff's first meeting for this purpose:

- "Imagine that this school year has already passed. What things would you like to look back on as having happened?"
- "It's a year from now. In your imagination, look back and identify those things that have happened which benefited the school program."
- "Imagine that you met a fellow teacher from another school a year from now. Think about what you would like to be able to tell him about the good things that happened to you during the past year at school."

If you are leading this meeting, you should consider asking the above questions for two and three years hence. A future orientation helps a group to get beyond excessive concern for current problems.

3.152   Each person clarifies own personal goals

During the initial staff meeting for goal setting, each member of the staff will be encouraged to identify his or her own personal goals. In the context of the above future orientation, ask the people in your group to make a list of items which:

a. Include the kind of experiences they would like to have during the year with other staff, children, and parents.

b. Identify the areas in which they would like to increase their own skills, knowledge, understanding, abilities, and awareness during the coming year.

c. Sort out priorities, so that each person indicates which items are most important; which are short-term or long-term wishes.

The purposes of this exercise are to:

a. Focus attention on those goals (including wishes, hopes, and desires) which most directly apply to each teacher's work at school.

b. Seek to identify which personal goals most closely articulate with the overall needs of the school.

3.153   Small groups identify common visions

After each person has completed the task of the last section, and the future orientation is firmly established in the group, divide the staff into random groups of six to eight persons. Within each group, every member (in turn) will verbally share her goal list with the group. The goal of this exercise is to identify the ideas, goals, or visions that are commonly held by most members in the group. This exercise will also allow members of the staff to know each other personally, as well as moving toward clarifying mutually held goals.

The following are important considerations:

• Have large sheets of paper (and felt-tipped pens) available so that the various items can be listed for all to see. One member of each group should act as a recorder.

• Since each person has a unique way of identifying personal goals, it is necessary to leave sufficient time for discussion and clarification in this exercise. One to one-and-a-half hours should be allowed for it.

• Certain rules should guide the discussion in the small groups:

a. No critical comments are made about anyone's ideas.
b. No evaluative comments are made about any idea.
c. Questions that are required to clarify an idea are permitted.
d. The group does not select ideas because they are good, but only because most people share the idea, or one very similar.

This is how the group can agree on common goals:

1. As each person shares her list of items with the small group, all other members of the group should compare the items to their own.

2. Alongside each of their own items, a notation should be made regarding similarity. Place an (S) beside items that are the same or quite similar; place an (R) beside items that refer to the same issue; place an (A) beside items that fall into the same general area.

3. It is permissible to ask questions of each group member in order to clarify. By the time each person in the group has shared her list, all members of the group should have noted which of their items are similar to others, and to what degree, by reviewing the number of notations alongside each item.

4. The group then identifies those items that are most common in the group. These are listed on butcher paper, in a summary form that is agreed to by the group.

5. After listing the five or six issues that are most common in the group, they are then rank-ordered by the group, through discussion, in terms of greatest importance.

6. The above issues should be re-stated as goals which conform to the models of goal statements which are described above. These are then listed on butcher paper for presentation to the whole staff.

3.154 Feedback and clarification to large group

The people from the small groups then return to the larger group.

• Each small group selects one communicator who will present their agreed-upon goal statements to the total group.

• This person will answer questions or direct them to other members of the small group.

• All of the goal statements of each small group should be posted together so that similarities among the lists are apparent.

• The total staff, by reviewing the posted lists, can then arrive at a list of the most commonly held goals. Agreement can be arrived at through discussion or through the accordion method (see Section 9.422).

3.155 Staff picks those goals on which they agree

The teaching staff at Solomon Elementary School was looking for some central themes for the coming year. The school administrator, Mrs. Siker, had spent most of the past school year suggesting the need for the staff to work together more actively. Recent discussions about school accountability had made many teachers concerned about the lack of clarity about what they wanted to accomplish.

Mrs. Siker and the teachers agreed to spend one day together, prior to the opening of school, to see if they could agree on a direction for the year.

Using the goal-setting procedures described above, three subgroups developed lists of goals.

When the lists were displayed before the whole staff, a lively discussion ensued. At first there seemed to be too much diversity among the goals for any central theme to arise, until it was pointed out that several items seemed to be related. A teacher stated that what it suggested to him was something about self-esteem. His statement was agreed to by the staff. After further discussion, the staff agreed to have a subcommittee of four meet over lunch, and try to put together the various suggestions.

After lunch the staff reconvened to hear the report. Mrs. Fletcher, the librarian, had put together a chart of recommendations.

Overall goal for the year: "To improve the self-image of children (and staff) at Solomon School."

Goals derived from the above:

a. To increase the number of activities that will help children have higher self-esteem.

b. To improve the interpersonal climate at the school.

The subcommittee showed how many of the original goals were included in this listing. The staff approved the new goal definition, and then considered other recommendations of the subcommittee.

1. Divide the staff into three work groups, by interest—one for each goal.

2. Have an inservice program early in the school year on the subject of self-esteem and self-image.

3. Devote the rest of the staff's day to developing some objectives for each goal.

The staff agreed and got to work.

3.2 DEFINING OBJECTIVES

Having specific objectives serves to keep a staff on target in any educational program. The following material will help you and your staff reach consensus about them.

3.21 How Objectives Differ from Goals

While goals are broad statements of (usually) long-range purposes, objectives are statements that define measurable, observable behavior that leads toward a goal. Whereas goals have an indeterminate life span, objectives define time limits precisely.

3.22 How Objectives Are Related to Goals

A goal is analogous to a mountain peak, in that there may be many paths to reach it. A well-stated goal can be reached through a variety of programs. Just as periodic landmarks indicate progress in a path toward the summit, so objectives serve as indices of how well the program is progressing toward a goal.

The selection of objectives should always be in accordance with the resources and capabilities of the person or group that is attempting to reach a goal. When determining objectives, the following questions should be asked:

- What observable behavior will tell that we are moving toward a goal?
- What observable behavior will tell that we are receding from a goal?
- What can we do to reach a goal that is within our resources and capabilities?

3.23 Why Are Objectives Important?

Objectives lend concrete reality to what are often vague hopes that are contained in goal statements. They allow people to define experiences that can measurably determine whether there is movement toward a goal.

A well-stated objective will provide specific guidelines for activities and programs, and will clarify what it is that people must do to reach a goal.

3.24 What Makes a Good Objective?

Poor objectives can lead to confusion, and undermine a group's intention to accomplish a goal. A poor objective tends to increase ambiguity rather than reduce it.

A good objective contains four elements. They are:

1. WHAT will be accomplished.
2. WHO the persons are whose behavior will be measured.
3. WHEN the specified behavior will be measured.
4. HOW MUCH of the behavior will show that some standard has been reached.

3.241 WHAT—the action to be completed

This part of an objective can be any of the following things:

- taking a test, e.g., a reading test
- the absence of a previously observed behavior, e.g., fighting on the playground

- the presence of a new behavior, e.g., students helping each other in class
- the performance of a particular task, e.g., counting to 10
- the completion of a concrete product, e.g., finish the Manual of School Rules

3.242   WHO—the target group

This part of an objective can be any of the following:

- everyone, e.g., the average score of all children taking a test
- part of a group, e.g., the intermediate grade teachers
- a special segment of a larger group, e.g., all children scoring over one year or more below grade level on a survey test
- a person, e.g., Sara

3.243   WHEN—time

This part of an objective can be any of the following:

- a specific date, e.g., June 30th
- a contingent date, e.g., three months after a test is given
- far away, e.g., one year hence
- close up, e.g., in two weeks

3.244   HOW MUCH—at what standard

This part of an objective can be any of the following:

- a score on a test, e.g., grade level on a math test
- a relative reduction in something, e.g., half as many fights reported to the principal
- a relative increase in something, e.g., twice as many books checked out of the library
- an absolute number of something, e.g., 30 reading lessons completed

3.25   Examples of Educational Objectives

Some examples of educational objectives are:

• 75% of the 4th grade children	WHO
will score above grade level	HOW MUCH
on a standardized reading test	WHAT
administered in May.	WHEN
• All teachers	WHO
by May 1st	WHEN
will complete a list of goals for the coming year	WHAT
which will include three objectives in each major curriculum area.	HOW MUCH

• The number of reported incidences of fighting	WHAT
among upper grade children	WHO
will be reduced to half of those recorded in June	HOW MUCH
by December, 1977.	WHEN

3.26 Procedures for Defining Objectives

STEP I—After the staff has agreed on one or more goal statements, divide into small groups, each focusing on one goal.

STEP II—Each small group will brainstorm "behavioral indices" that would show that a goal has been reached. They should ask the question, "What things might be observed if this goal was reached?" There will be many answers placed on butcher paper, so the group can keep track of its answers.

STEP III—After completing the previous step, look at the variety of items and select several of them, using the following criteria:

a. Is it an important behavioral change?
b. Is it measurable?
c. Can it be observed in some way?
d. Is it really an "indicator" of the goal?

STEP IV—The small list that results from the previous step will become the WHAT of one or more objectives. At this time, the group should begin to identify the WHO—the target group for whom the objective is defined (see Section 3.242).

STEP V—Consider the WHEN. It may be reasonable to define a target date at this stage, and it should be considered. It is often more useful, however, to delay setting a target date until program activities are clarified, so that enough time is allowed for everything to get done.

STEP VI—defining the HOW MUCH part of an objective may involve expert advice about evaluation and measurement. It also means that the group must reach consensus on reasonable expectations of the target group's performance. You should consider the following procedure:

a. Have the group brainstorm ideas about evaluation and expectations. List the various ideas.
b. Select a small group to work with you, the school psychologist, or someone familiar with measurement evaluation.
c. Have this smaller group sift through the ideas, clarify measurement procedures and level of performance expectations, and report to the staff at a later date with well-formed objectives for staff discussion.

STEP VII—When objectives are completed, the total staff should review them for clarity and reasonableness, making any adjustments required.

3.3 USING PROBLEM-SOLVING PROCEDURES IN PLANNING PROGRAMS

Agreeing on an effective plan is looked at as a "problem." The solution to the problem *is* a plan of action.

3.31 Refer to Chapter 2 on Problem Solving

The steps to follow when developing programs to carry out your objectives are described in the previous chapter.

3.32 How to Complete the Objective Is the Problem

By following the procedures for clarifying goals and objectives, you have, in effect, "created a problem for yourselves." Finding your method for completing the objective is the "problem" you have to solve. The rest of the problem-solving steps will help you work out activities on which you and your staff agree.

3.33 How to Use Time-Lines as a Planning Technique

You may already be familiar with "time-lines." A time-line is a calendar of events, which lays out a series of activities that lead to some anticipated event.

The time-line can also be a planning tool. It can be used creatively at the stage in the planning process when objectives have clearly been stated. The features of using time-line planning are as follows:

a. You plan "backward" in time! And forward, too.
b. The planning can occur in a group setting, in which all can participate.
c. People need to have clarity and agreement on the objective, and some idea of the things that may be required to get to it.
d. You only need to ask three questions of each stage:
   • What must immediately precede the anticipated event in order for it to occur?
   • Who must do it?
   • When must it be done?

3.331 An example of time-line plan

Start with your objective: By May, 75% of children in grades 3-6 will show one year's increase on a standardized reading test. All children will have been tested by the same instrument in September, to establish the base line.

Brainstorm some things that will probably occur:

Tests given in September and May.
Develop new approaches to reading.
Procure supplementary materials.
Have special inservice for teachers.
Have consultant in reading.
Develop parent interest and support.
Evaluate progress periodically.
Make time for inservice session.

Think about persons or groups that will be involved in the program, and make a list of those:

All teachers in grades 3-6
Reading Consultant
Administrator
Reading Project Committee
Aides
Parent Volunteers

After the group has done the above (remember, brainstorm—see Section 2.41), you are ready to start your time-line.

• Make a calendar on a large sheet of roll paper. Have a column for each month from now to the month the objective is completed.

• In the rows, list those people or groups who are likely to participate. Leave space for others whom you might not anticipate.

• The calendar should look like this, the one in Figure 3-1.

	Sept.	Oct.	Nov.	Dec.	Jan.	Feb.	March	Apr.	May
Teachers grades 3-6									
Reading Consultants									
Administrator									
Project Committee									
Aides									
Parent Volunteers									

FIGURE 3-1

Now, you are ready to fill in the time-line. Keep your list of probable activities posted so that the group can refer to it.

You begin, and continue to ask yourselves a series of questions, as shown in Figure 3-2.

1. What action must occur in May?	1. The reading test is administered.
2. By whom?	2. Teachers in grades 3-6.
3. In order for them to do it, what must happen?	3. They need the tests.
4. By when?	4. The beginning of May.
5. Who will get them the tests?	5. The Project Committee.
6. When should the Committee have the tests?	6. In April.
7. Who should order the tests?	7. The Administrator.
8. When?	8. Early enough to be on time.
9. What preparation for the tests should occur?	9. Children should have increased experience in reading.
10. When should this happen?	10. Throughout the year.
11. Who should give them their experience?	11. All teachers in grades 3-6.
12. How will they do this?	12. Through inservice training program.
13. When will this occur?	13. One session per month, Oct.-March.
14. Who will provide the inservice?	14. A Reading Consultant.
15. Who will provide the Consultant?	15. Project Committee and Administrator.
16. When will he/she be hired?	16. Before October.
17. What else needs to be done to accomplish #9?	17. Supplementary reading materials need to be procured.
18. Who will do this?	18. All teachers (individually).
19. How will they do this?	19. Based on recommendations of Consultant and Project Committee.
20. When will this be done?	20. By November.
21. How?	21. Standard requisitions turned into office.
22. How will teachers know how much to spend?	22. Administrator will inform them.
23. When?	23. By October, based on firm budget figures.

FIGURE 3-2

24. (*Refer to #12.*) Who will participate in inservice?

24. All teachers and aides.

25. (*See list.*) What about Parent Volunteers?

25. Need lots of them in order to individualize.

26. Who will recruit them?

26. Administrator (*loud groan*).

27. When?

27. Early in year (Sept.-Oct.)

28. How?

28. Announcements and special event.

29. What special event?

29. Open House in Oct.

30. What announcement?

30. Newsletter about Reading Project.

31. When?

31. In September.

32. Who will prepare it?

32. Project Committee.

33. When?

33. Early in September.

34. How will parent volunteers help?

34. By working with individual children who need help.

35. How will they know how to do this?

35. Train them.

36. Who will do it?

36. Project Committee (*loud groan*).

37. How?

37. Workshop and follow-up session.

38. When?

38. End of October, and bi-monthly refresher.

39. Where?

39. At school.

40. Who will design workshop?

40. Project Committee, Administrator, and Consultant.

41. When?

41. Early in October.

42 (*Look at original list of activities.*) When will periodic evaluation occur?

42. At inservice in December and February.

43. How will this happen?

43. Teachers will: (1) Interim reading progress data through test. (2) Share activities they are doing. (3) Discuss problems.

44. In order for that to happen, what must precede it?

44. Teachers need time to prepare.

45. How?

45. Additional minimum day.

46. When?

46. One week before evaluation session.

47. What will they need?

47. Interim testing materials.

48. Who will provide them?

48. Project Committee.

49. HAVE WE LEFT ANYTHING OUT?

49. YES.

FIGURE 3-2 *(continued)*

50. What?	50. Procure test for initial testing.
51. Who should do this?	51. Administrator.
52. When?	52. Early September.
53. What test?	53. Use standard District test.
54. HAVE WE LEFT ANY-THING OUT?	54. Don't think so.
55. ARE WE FINISHED?	55. For the time being. Add later on as needed.

FIGURE 3-2 (continued)

Either as you have been moving through this process, or at the end, the information developed should be placed in the time-line. When it is done, it should look like Figure 3-3, which is a detailed diagram of who must do what, when—in order to accomplish the objective.

3.332 What to do with the time-line

Some things to be done with the time-line are:

• Post final copies in teachers' room and administrator's office.
• Extra copies to relevant persons.
• Revise time-line when program gets under way, as needed.
• Specify dates for meetings, etc., as they are decided, and add to time-line.
• Add new features as they become necessary.

3.4 CREATING STAFF ORGANIZATION FOR PLANNING

When your staff understands and practices good planning procedures, the benefits will accrue for many years at your school. This section will point out many things you can do to insure effective, ongoing planning.

3.41 Convincing Staff About the Importance of Good Planning

If your staff has had frustrating experiences in planning activities, or if such activities are new ones, you may have to convince them that it's worthwhile.

3.411 Ways to demonstrate the value of good planning

Some ways of demonstrating the value of good planning are:
• Use good planning procedures yourself, and allow staff to observe you do it in staff meetings.

	SEPT	OCT	NOV	DEC	JAN	FEB	MARCH	APRIL	MAY
Teachers Grades 3-6		Inservice session one/month.	Develop new reading activities (10). →						Administer reading test (1)
			Order supplementary reading materials (18).	Evaluation session (42). Minimum Day.		Evaluation Session (42). Minimum Day			Get tests (4)
Administrator	Select consultant (15). Newsletter to parents (27). Procure tests (52).	INFORM teachers about budget (23). Open House for parents about Project (29). Prepare Parent Workshop (40).					Order tests (7)		

FIGURE 3-3

87

	SEPT	OCT	NOV	DEC	JAN	FEB	MARCH	APRIL	MAY
Project Committee	Select consultant (15). Prepare Parent Newsletter (33).	Recommend supplementary materials (20). Prepare and implement Parent Workshop (40).	Procure interim testing materials (48).		Procure interim testing materials (48).			Procure tests (6).	
Aides		Participate in inservice sessions.							
Parent Volunteers		Parent Workshop (38).		Workshop (38).		Workshop (38).		Workshop (38).	
Consultant		Conduct Inservice. Recommend supplementary materials (20).							

FIGURE 3-3 (continued)

• When it is necessary for the staff to make a decision together, always be sure that *what*, *how*, *who*, and *when* are made clear.

• Prepare detailed agendas for staff meetings. The staff will appreciate *your* good planning.

• Become familiar with another school that has engaged in group planning. Invite representatives from that school to share their experience with your staff.

• Use examples from this Handbook to demonstrate the procedures and outcomes of effective planning.

• Prepare a calendar of future events. Keep it posted in the staff room. Use it as a reference for the staff.

3.412   Motivating staff

Some methods of motivating your staff are:

• Increase opportunities for staff (as a whole or subgroups) to be involved in decisions.

• Express your interest in foreseeing crises and planning for them, rather than dealing with them when they occur.

• See Section 6.512 on building connectiveness among staff.

• Be sure that when decisions are made by staff, you monitor the follow-through. Having decisions actually carried out increases motivation.

• You must be convinced about the benefits of good planning. Your optimism will influence staff.

• Provide continuous feedback to staff about the status of decisions they have made. Keep notes of staff meetings for this purpose.

• Make meetings a pleasant experience. Coffee and refreshments, along with an informal atmosphere, will help.

• When contemplating a planning session, attempt to clarify beforehand the procedures to be used, the time involved, and the expected outcomes.

• If you have some teachers on your staff who use good planning procedures in their classrooms, encourage them to share these with the rest of the staff.

• Once planning activities begin, if the substance of them is of real interest to staff, the task itself becomes absorbing. Trust it.

3.42   Setting Up Task Forces, Committees, or Planning Groups

When setting up task-forces, committees, or planning groups, remember to:

• Attempt to have such groups be representative of the grades, specialties, or resources involved.

• Define, and commit to writing, the specific task or objective for the group.

• Clarify the authority of the group. What decisions can it make; what decisions must be referred to administration or the whole staff?

• Select members of the group so that persons with special expertise or interest are on it. Smaller groups of interested members are more effective than larger ones with disinterested members.

• Post a list of groups and their members in the staff room so that people know who is responsible for what.

• Have each special group take minutes of all meetings. Either distribute or post them, or have regular reports from them at staff meetings.

• Encourage staff members to participate equitably in such groups. Avoid having some staff members overcommitted.

• Clarify how long such groups should be in existence. Have them be task-oriented. Dissolve the group when its task is completed.

• Seek staff agreement on the importance of having everyone participate in some group during the year.

• See Section 4.41 on the different types of committees.

3.43   Administrator's Role in Planning

One of the ways in which you provide educational leadership in your school is by helping your staff use the resources of creativity, imagination, and expertise that its members possess. Effective planning permits those resources to be expressed in functional ways.

3.431   Delegating authority and responsibility

If an administrator gives a person or group responsibility for getting a job done and does not give the authority to make decisions and control resources, he risks undermining the morale of the group. This is ultimately destructive of a group's effectiveness.

Much authority for decisions in your school rests in your position. It is there either as an inherent function of your role as administrator, or you are delegated to carry out responsibilities defined by a higher authority, e.g., central office, the school board. In order to encourage your staff to take responsibility for providing quality education, you must take the risk of delegating to them some kinds of authority for making decisions and controlling resources. How much of this occurs depends on your personality, district policy, law, and the form of organization that you develop.

People are going to judge you by the way your staff handles the authority/ responsibility issue. You have a personal/professional interest in seeing that they handle it well.

The following things should be considered:

• Authority is the delegated ability to make decisions and control resources. Responsibility involves a mandate to complete a task. Each time a task is defined, there should be clarification of what decisions are required to do it, and what resources are needed.

• Realistically, you cannot take responsibility for everything that happens in your school. Others already have authority. The limits of your control need to be made clear.

• When you request staff to take responsibility, it is important to let them know *at the same time* what authority they will have.

• Awareness of effective decision-making, problem-solving, and planning techniques will insure responsible use of delegated authority.

• Encourage staff to discuss these issues when relevant.

• Your active participation in group planning allows you to monitor staff activities.

• Don't assume staff members fully understand the limits *or* possibilities of their authority. Take the lead in clarifying them.

• Ask your staff (in effect), "How far do you want to go?" Create a climate in which they can ask (in effect), "How far can we go?"

3.432   Clarifying constraints and limits

As the school's administrator, you will have more information than anyone else about the limitations on what can be done in your school. Limitations exist in all of the following areas:

a. Legal—What is permitted or disallowed under existing laws involving schools?

b. Financial—What money is available and how can it be used?

c. Time—What can reasonably be done in a given time period, and what other things must also fill that time?

d. Personnel—Who's available to do what, when?

e. Policies—What are they? Who made them? For what purpose? How do they influence your school?

f. Goals—What should be done? What's most important?

g. Physical—What do you have to work with? What can be done to change your plant? How can it be done?

An important function of your role is to clarify the limitations that impinge on the authority you give your staff. Clarifying such constraints early in any planning process can help in setting realistic goals and objectives. Your staff will look to you for this information. They will also look for your leadership in overcoming such limitations.

3.433 Supporting, encouraging and influencing

Here are some ways you can support, encourage and influence your staff:
• Delegating authority and responsibility to staff teams or committees permits you to work with smaller groups on specific problems. By doing so, you can influence the problem-solving process.
• Encourage people to elaborate on ideas that they raise in meetings.
• Show appreciation for a person's participation as well as ideas.
• Facilitate discussion of controversial points in meetings.
• Recognize individuals' special talents or knowledge. Find ways to use such qualities in the group's work.
• Avoid throwing your weight around. Express your feelings or ideas as such, not as authoritative pronouncements.
• Avoid lobbying with individuals who are members of committees. Bring your ideas or concerns to the whole group.
• Make an overt agreement with the staff that you, as administrator, have the right to participate in any planning group at any time.
• The most important kind of support and encouragement comes about through your active effort to provide the resources that planning teams need in order to do their job.

3.5 DANGERS TO AVOID, AND HOW

Effective planning can break down, even within a highly motivated staff, if certain dangers are overlooked. The following sections point out some of these dangers.

3.51 Trying to Do Too Much

Developing too many plans, having too many goals, and underestimating the amount of time required are common failings in the planning process. Apart from the ordinary work of a teaching staff, a school usually cannot comfortably handle more than one or two special programs in which all staff are involved. The following issues should be considered:
• It is important to monitor and evaluate progress in working toward a goal. Be sure to include interim evaluations in your plan. By setting times for these, in your plan, you can more readily judge the overall time commitment.
• Some goals and objectives should be for more than one year. There is a

tendency to try to accomplish everything in one year. The more global the goal, the longer it takes to accomplish it. Set objectives for varying time periods.

• Try to consider as many contingencies as possible ahead of time. People often forget to plan around holidays, special administrative tasks, other programs, etc. When such events occur unexpectedly, they throw off careful planning, get you behind schedule, and result in frustration.

• One good index of the workability of a plan is the relative quantity of required resources that are currently available within the system. Every time a resource is needed that is not readily available, the risk of unexpected contingencies arising increases. When you need lots of resources that you don't have, it may mean that you're trying to do too much.

3.52 Setting Unreasonably High Standards

The staff of Kennedy Elementary had been concerned about improving reading scores in the third through sixth grades for several years. Different reading programs had not done the trick, and there had been little educational leadership from the administrator. The most recent testing had shown that children at Kennedy were, on the average, 12 months below state norms.

A new administrator was assigned to Kennedy. Mrs. Anthony came with high recommendations from her previous school—as an educational innovator.

One change that staff liked was their increased participation in planning. The reading problem was given the highest priority, and it was decided to launch an intensive effort to improve reading scores during the year.

Given the combination of the staff's enthusiasm and Mrs. Anthony's zeal, plans were laid for parental involvement, individualized reading instruction, new materials, and consulting help. The district agreed to lay out the increased expenses. With this arsenal of resources, the staff decided to reach for a high standard in the reading program. Their objective was to advance *all* children at least nine months during the year, with an *average* reading improvement of 12 months for all children in grades 3-6.

As the year progressed, the interim evaluations showed improvement, but by February, the children were "peaking out." The scores in March indicated an average reading growth of six months for the school. Many children had not improved significantly. It was apparent that the objective would not be met.

Several staff meetings were devoted to trying to find out why more had not occurred. Some teachers were accused of not having done everything they could. Important materials had arrived late. Fewer parents than anticipated participated as tutors. A flu epidemic lasted more than a month, and Mrs. Anthony had been out for a month because of minor surgery.

It was finally agreed that the initial enthusiasm was excessive. There was considerable improvement in reading overall, but the sour taste remained for some time, since the staff had not met the standard it set for itself.

3.53 Frustration and Blaming When Objectives Are Not Met

People will vary in the intensity of commitment to a goal, even though they participated in setting the goal or objective. When an objective is not being met, those with a greater commitment will have become more emotionally tied to it. This may result in blaming or seeking some scapegoat for frustrated feelings. Often the scapegoat is the administrator.

In order to avoid this, keep in mind the following:

• An objective should not be used like the rabbit at a dog track—it keeps the dogs running, even though they can't catch it. Set reasonable objectives that are attainable.

• Objectives can and should be altered when it seems they might not be met. The group that sets it can change it.

• Not meeting an objective is an opportunity to reexamine the program for reaching it; this is an occasion for learning not to blame.

• Open communication and effective monitoring of programs are your best insurance against unanticipated constraints.

• See Chapters 4, on conflict resolution, and 9, on communications.

3.54 Losing Interest

There are several reasons why a staff loses interest in things it planned to do:

• Unless some action occurs soon after the planning is done, interest will flag because other interests and conditions can intervene.

• Unanticipated conditions can distract the staff. Many could have been anticipated if time was devoted to foreseeing them.

• Plans that span the summer run serious risk of the above, especially if planning is done in spring but nothing happens until fall.

• When people lose track of where they are or what is happening, interest can wane. Frequent feedback and evaluation keep interest high.

• Too much time elapsing between significant events can allow people to forget where they are going. Use time-line planning to insure a regular incidence of events.

• If some activity in a program cannot be done, people may feel that the plan is failing. Either promote a substitute activity or discuss the consequences, which may not be great.

• A staff that has been traditionally crisis-oriented will tend to have a short attention span. You can introduce effective planning practices to increase involvement.

3.55 Disparaging Small Gains

People with high standards often get discouraged if small gains do not measure up to those standards. People on your staff will vary in the way they apply standards. Your support and encouragement can do much to smooth out such frustrations.

Always emphasize that dissatisfactions that arise in the planning/action process are always occasions for reexamination of what is being done. This is a safety valve all through the planning procedures.

3.6   AN EXAMPLE OF A SIMPLE PLANNING PROCEDURE—CREATING AN EFFECTIVE DISCIPLINE PROGRAM FOR YOUR SCHOOL

The following procedure can be used to create an effective and humane discipline program, when the following conditions have been met:

1. A majority of staff feel that student behavior is a problem, though they may not agree on all aspects.

2. The staff is willing to spend four to six hours working *together* on it. The staff can agree to delegate the procedure to a subcommittee.

3. The administrator is willing to participate in the process.

The goal is to develop a clear set of expectations for behavior, and consequences for misbehavior that will be communicated to children and parents. Staff agreement and consistency are also important outcomes.

Preliminary procedures:

a. Have large sheets of paper and broad felt-tipped pens at hand.
b. Divide the staff into groups of four to six, randomly.
c. Have each group select a secretary and discussion leader.
d. Time: two to three hours for the first session.

3.61 Identifying the Problem Areas

Directive: Each group, working independently, is to identify the areas in the school where behavior problems exist.

Procedure:

a. Each small group is to list those areas in which its members feel that problems exist. Examples:

corridors	bathrooms
lunch room	classrooms
office	playground
multi-use room	gymnasium
bus stop	library
(others)	

b. The secretary lists on paper those areas agreed to by the small group as having problems.

c. After 20 minutes, post the sheets for all to see.

d. Point out those areas in which several groups agree that problems exist. Select the most important problem areas.

e. Each group takes one area to work on in the next two steps.

3.62   Identifying the Problem Behaviors

Directive: Each group, working independently, is to describe problem behaviors in their area. Only behaviors are to be listed, not attitudes, feelings, or causes.

Procedure:

a. List the behaviors that are problems. Examples:

running	shouting
hitting	food throwing
back-talking	tearing books
shoving	jumping
unauthorized use of equipment	(others)

b. Note how they are done, who does them, and other features of time and circumstance.

c. List the results on a sheet of paper.

3.63   Clarify Desired Behaviors

Directive: Each group is to clarify the ways students *should* act in each area.

Procedure:

a. List the behaviors that are desired. Examples:

walk	keep hands to self
avoid fighting	return trays
line up quietly	do not shout
stay off equipment	(others)

b. List on a sheet of paper.

c. When Sections 3.162 and 3.163 have been done, post sheets and have one member of each group report what was done to the entire staff.

d. Elicit comments or suggestions from staff. Simply note them for future use.

3.64   Develop Ways to Reinforce Desired Behaviors

At this stage, each group acts as a planning group. They are to develop ways to reinforce the behavior identified in Section 3.63 above. These should include individual and group rewards that can be easily identified and earned by the children. Examples:

- Special recognition for groups that behave well.
- Special treats for good lunchroom behavior.
- Extended recesses for good playground behavior.
- Principal gives special commendations.

Programs for reinforcing desired behavior should be approved by total staff, and a planning group established to work out details, using the planning procedures described in this chapter.

Punishing for misbehavior without reinforcing good behavior takes longer to change the school climate, and will tend to create a repressive atmosphere.

3.65   Consequences That Are Graduated in Severity

Since not all children will respond to positive reinforcers, sanctions for chronic offenders are required. If programs developed for Section 3.64 work well, the sanctions developed here will need to be applied fairly. Examples of graduated consequences:

	a.	b.	c.
1st offense:	(1) Written citation to parent	(2) Verbal warning and citation	(3) Teacher pupil con- ference

2nd offense:	(1) Teacher-parent conference	(2) Isolation in class	(3) Principal-pupil conference
3rd offense:	(1) Principal-parent conference	(2) Parent notification	(3) Parents informed
4th offense:	(1) Suspension	(2) Parent-teacher conference	(3) Principal, parent, and student conference

3.66 Communicating Expectations, Standards, and Procedures

The above process is complete when all aspects of behavior that are (or might become) concerns to the staff are analyzed. A body of material will have been developed which can be organized into a *Manual of School Behavior*. Completing this is best done by a subcommittee of the staff. Final approval by the whole staff is suggested.

A simplified version of this Manual should be sent to all parents. If there is a Parent Advisory Group, it should have the opportunity to review it.

All teachers should present the material to their classes (usually in several sections), and classroom discussions about behavior should be held. The reinforcers and consequences (see Sections 3.64 and 3.65) should be clearly described to the students.

3.7 EVALUATING THE DISCIPLINE PROGRAM

Form a team whose function is to periodically evaluate the effectiveness of the discipline procedures. The team's evaluation needs to be conveyed to the total staff.

The features that should be looked at are:

a. The change in frequency of misbehavior.
b. The satisfaction of the staff with the procedures.
c. The consistency of the staff in imposing the consequences.
d. The satisfaction of the children with the reinforcers.

4

How to Resolve Conflicts

Schools can become seed-beds in which conflict can germinate and flourish. They bring together people who play different but important roles in a child's life, who need to resolve differences in order to develop a unified approach to children's education.

Many people, both educators and parents, use the school as an arena in which to work out personal power issues with the broader democratic society. The schools, for many, are the most intimate interface with the "power structures"—government, bureaucracy, and the professions. The tradition of local control has existed for so long in the United States that many people feel it is their responsibility to exercise personal influence on the schools.

As the teaching profession becomes more militant; as schools seek parent participation; and as the community finds that school is one of the few public institutions that can be significantly influenced by citizen action—it is difficult to avoid conflicts.

Finding compromises with which people can live (consensus) is the goal of conflict resolution. The school administrator must assume a central role in this task. In this chapter you will find:

- How to recognize sources of conflict in a school.
- Principles of how to resolve conflict.
- Case studies describing methods for working with the characteristic dilemmas you face.
- When to use questionnaires and surveys to help you gather information about actual or potential conflicts.

Note to the Reader:

There is important information about methods of dealing with conflict contained in—

4.1 SOURCES OF CONFLICT IN A SCHOOL COMMUNITY

In this section a number of characteristic conflicts that occur within schools are analyzed. Approaches for handling these conflicts are suggested.

4.11 Source of Conflict—Differences in Educational Objectives

Educational objectives are those things that we want children *to do*, *to be*, or *to have* as a result of going to school. Differences among people in philosophy, socio-economic status, and tradition insure that there will be some disagreement about educational objectives. These differences often result in polarization about a limited number of broad objectives, i.e., basic skills vs. enrichment; creative development vs. emphasis on academic subjects; sciences vs. arts. For example:

At a suburban school in California, which had recently adopted the Early Childhood Education (ECE) program, considerable conflict arose among the parents over the program's objectives. Some wished to see an emphasis placed on teaching basic skills in a structured environment; others argued heatedly that young children needed to learn how to get along with each other and to be creative. After many meetings between staff and parents, a compromise was reached: parents would be given a choice among some classes that emphasized the basics and others that exemplified the open-classroom approach of the ECE program.

The administrator of a school in which conflict about objectives is current (or potential) must take steps to head off the formation of divisive subgroups within the school. He can do this by:

Step 1: Uncovering the priorities held by various segments of the community.
Step 2: Providing feedback to all about the views held.
Step 3: Creating arenas for discussion.

Surveys that gather objective information can provide a basis for discussion (see Sections 1.13, 2.211, 3.15, 4.5 and 7.31). If substantial disagreements are uncovered, open discussions will allow the school to consider all viewpoints (see Sections 7.8, 9.0, 4.41).

4.12 Source of Conflict—Value Differences

Values are a mixture of what people consciously believe (and can state), and what they feel (but cannot put into words). Because of this mixture of feeling and belief, talking about values can become either overly abstract or intensely personal.

Changing people's values is always difficult and frequently impossible. To try to do so is *not* a reasonable goal for a school administrator. *The goal is to create a climate in which tolerance for differences becomes a commonly held value.*

In order to do this, you must be a model for tolerance of alternative values (see Sections 6.34 and 8.6). You must provide many opportunities for people to get together. You must bring the issue of value differences into a more objective framework, i.e., discussion of programs and activities.

People must be able to see the *possibility* of having their values influence the school's program (see Sections 1.14, 1.2, 3.4 and 6.33).

4.13 Source of Conflict—Personality

If "personality" were the issue, then everyone would be in conflict with everyone else a good part of the time. It is *not* a reasonable strategy to try to change a person's personality as a way of resolving a conflict. This issue of personality conflict is a result of one or more of the following factors:

• People have differing needs. Some need to have situations structured and defined; others need flexibility and looseness. Everyone seeks to organize his life so as to fulfill personal needs. When needs differ, people will disagree about goals.

• People's previous experiences influence new situations. Attitudes, feelings, and hopes from the past continually affect the present and visions of the future.

• Everyone seeks to improve his sense of self-worth, and will use all resources toward this end. What makes one person feel good about himself, may make another feel bad.

• When people's needs, talents, or wishes do not fit the roles they fill, discomfort and frustration occur. If someone believes that he is an excellent fifth grade teacher, but must teach kindergarten, resentment and frustration may affect his relations with others, as well as his job performance.

Personal discussions with those who are party to a conflict are necessary (see Sections 1.14, 7.63 and 8.6).

You must translate the "problem" of personality into the above factors. Then identify where and how to assist.

4.14 Source of Conflict—Staff and Administration Conflicts

There is a basic paradox about authority in our schools. While we tend to mistrust authority and suspect abuses of power, we also believe that those in authority should effectively perform their functions in the interests of those they serve.

You are caught on the horns of this dilemma. You are often expected to use your authority to make the decisions that others want you to make.

Conflicts between staff and administration fall into one or more of the following categories:

1. *Struggles for power—who will make the decision?* Often, staff wants you to make the decision, while you want them to make it. This is really a conflict about "who will decide who decides."

2. *Fear of losing power—if you win, I lose.* Experience shows, however, that when power is shared, everyone experiences an increased sense of power.

3. *Confusion about who has the power.* Are you an administrator who conducts a democratic school in an autocratic manner? "I have decided that you *will* help me make decisions!" Or, do you manipulate while seeming democratic and open. "I need your approval for this, but if I don't get it, I'll find a way to pay you back!"

In order to avoid these pitfalls, it is necessary to maintain open communication, and to provide forums in which differences can be aired.

Creating effective problem-solving and decision-making procedures is the basis for mutual trust and respect.

You must be able to understand how your staff perceives you, and what you can do to improve your relationship to them (see Sections 1.2, 4.4, 9.2 and 10.3).

Confusion about who has authority is a function of confusion about roles. Role clarity is necessary to resolve many dilemmas about power (see Chapter 10).

4.15 Source of Conflict—Differing Expectations About Children's Behavior

Most conflicts about children's behavior indicate disagreements about one or more of the following questions:

1. How much personal responsibility can be expected from children?
2. Is home or school more responsible for a child's behavior at school?
3. What standards will be used to judge appropriate behavior?
4. How much variation in behavior is tolerable?
5. Who cares more—parents or teachers?
6. Who knows more—parents, teachers, or the administrator?
7. Are children "good" and need to be free; are they "bad" and need to be constrained?
8. How much can a child be expected to learn?

Don't try to convince people that they are "wrong" about children. Views about children are so closely related to one's own experiences that it is easy to stimulate irrationality by attacking people's beliefs in this area.

The goal must be to involve people (parents as well as teachers) in discussion about how they want children to behave, and to avoid philosophical debates. You will reach consensus about *what* to do if you can avoid arguing about *why* to do it.

It is always best to know what people think.

It is important to let parents know what the school is actually doing, so as to head off conflict based on misinformation (see Sections 7.2 and 7.3).

It is necessary to reach consensus, and initiate activities, rather than getting stuck in debates.

4.16   Source of Conflict—Skills and Resources Inadequate to Task

When we don't have the resources or capabilities to solve a problem, we usually feel frustrated, resentful and powerless (see Section 6.33). When teachers can't solve problems, meet objectives, or carry out programs, personal feelings contribute to a decline of the school climate. *When morale decreases, interpersonal conflict and mistrust increase.*

If staff or parents are encouraged to participate in decision making, they must have effective management skills (see Sections 3.4, 7.4, 7.9 and 9.4).

Helping staff members procure needed resources is one of your major functions.

Schools that have high work pressure (see Section 1.32), but must struggle for resources, will usually be seed-beds for conflict.

4.17   Source of Conflict—Disagreement Over Use of Limited Resources: Time, Money and Materials

It is no longer advisable, in most schools, for the administrator to *tell* people what they should have, yet participative decision making creates "lobbies" for resources that are needed for pet projects. Concerned teachers will fight for the things that will improve their classrooms. You, as an administrator, are called upon to parcel out the resources that are available—and must try to satisfy conflicting demands.

The antidote for these competitive struggles is a cooperative climate—in a school and its surrounding community—which this Handbook helps you create.

4.2 HOW TO RESOLVE CONFLICTS: BASIC PRINCIPLES

While it is important to know the basic principles of how to resolve conflicts, this *knowledge* alone is insufficient, for your *feelings* are involved. You must understand and retrain those feelings, which conflict stimulates in *you*, in order to put the principles into action (see Chapter 8). Nevertheless, they can guide your thinking and behavior.

4.21 Advantage of Trust Over Mistrust

It is easy to trust people who agree with you and keep their word, but it is difficult to trust someone who you feel has lied, or has not kept his word. When mistrust is present, to trust is risky; yet, by trusting you have more to gain than to lose. By trusting someone you help build the other's self-esteem, and/or activate guilt if he has broken a trust. This often makes it likely that he will keep his word the next time.

What do you do, however, when you have a great deal to lose? It is necessary to establish *conditions* whereby trust can be reestablished.

The following steps help to do this:

1. *Share feelings of discomfort.* "I'm feeling uneasy about giving you permission to take the children on this field trip. Last time several children were lost."

2. *Indicate the importance of the relationship to you and your desire to improve it.* "I would really like to see you and the children go on that field trip, but because of what happened last time maybe we could think through a plan that would satisfy both of us."

3. *Identify and clarify the problem and set up problem-solving procedures* (see Chapter 2 on Problem-Solving Procedures). "Let's see what made it difficult for the children to stay with the group last time."

4. *Arrive at a clear agreement about what each person will do and determine a way to verify whether the agreement has been kept.* Put these agreements in writing when possible, but be sure you've agreed to something you can live with. We often agree to things in order to placate the other person.

This gesture is a dangerous one because we've tried to avoid stress, rather than solve a problem. Before agreeing, ask yourself the following questions:

- Am I able to keep this agreement?
- If it is kept by both of us, will I feel good about it?
- Does something more need to be clarified?

It is very important when making agreements that both parties clarify what they've heard by paraphrasing and listening (see Section 4.22). Many agreements are not broken because of ill will. Often both parties conscientiously follow the agreements they thought they heard, but have actually misunderstood each other.

4.22 Clarify Feelings and Listen

An administrator in a northern California elementary school was frustrated because her teachers allowed children to run in the halls, despite agreements not to do this. Only after she had listened to the teachers' dissatisfaction with the way she disciplined children did the running stop. The administrator learned that people will often express anger by passive rebellion, rather than stating feelings directly.

When people state their feelings directly, solutions can be formed, and agreements can be made and kept. Give time to the expression of feelings. It will pay off in time saved in problem solving. Unexpressed feelings act as blocks to finding solutions. They *do* become expressed, but as vague resentments and frustrations (see Sections 2.14, 3.5, 5.2 and 8.6).

Here is how the administrator can help in getting feelings expressed:

- *Reflect feelings* that often lie hidden underneath the other person's statements. For example, a teacher says "Staff meetings are a waste of time." The administrator replies, "You feel frustrated at the way staff meetings are going." In this example, the administrator is paraphrasing the feelings behind the other person's statement.

- State your feelings as *your feelings*, and encourage others to share theirs. For example, the administrator says, "I, too, feel frustrated by the meetings because many of the staff are doing homework and not paying attention. I wonder what things in the meeting bother you, and how you feel about them?"

- Even if you do not agree with a person's opinion, indicate that you've heard them before disagreeing. Frequently people will just hammer harder for their point of view if they feel the other person has not heard it. For example: "As I understand it, you feel that staff meetings should be held only once a month. However, I feel that we need to have them more often, because there are a lot of problems at this school that need talking over."

• Help develop an expectation among staff that it is O.K. to express negative as well as positive feelings. One way to do this is to have an evaluation questionnaire at the end of some meetings, which encourages staff to freely express feelings.

4.23   Set Limits for Self and Others

Setting limits for yourself means being honest about your own limitations, capabilities, and resources. Setting limits for others means being clear about what behavior in others you cannot tolerate, and what you will do if such behavior continues.

Why is limit setting so important?

• If you're not clear about your own limits, then you will often make commitments that you cannot fulfill, which is frustrating for yourself and others. This frustration promotes further conflict.

• Setting limits for others is of critical importance. If they do not know the limits for their behavior with you, they will become anxious and often test limits inappropriately.

• Setting limits for yourself and others enhances your own self-respect.

If knowing your own limits and making them clear is a problem for you, see Section 8.4.

4.24   Clarify Responsibilities and Keep Agreements

Ambiguity and misunderstanding occur when people in a school are not clear about their responsibilities. Such misunderstandings result in accusations, blame, and attacks on personalities. Why might you have difficulty being clear about arguments and responsibilities?

• Most often it is because no clear agreements have been reached. There has been a minimal effort to be explicit, and you have had to work from assumptions, which often proved false.

• You may be reluctant to persist in clarifying agreements, for fear that you will seem to be compulsive, authoritarian, or unsure of yourself. Most people feel that they are more explicit than is actually the case, and don't like to be challenged.

• You may assume responsibility for how others feel. This often stems from an excessive concern with having others like you, or, perhaps, you've been taught to feel guilty when someone else makes a mistake. It is necessary to distinguish being *responsible* from being *concerned*. When you say, "I'm responsible," you feel that *you* ought to have the singular ability to affect events and to influence change. When you say, "I'm concerned," it indicates your desire to be more aware of how you affect others, and your willingness to *share* responsibility.

• You may be reluctant to hold others responsible for agreements they have made, because you avoid being assertive or don't wish to be authoritarian. On the other hand, many people are *not* aware of their responsibilities, and it takes someone insisting that they be responsible to make them aware of the importance of keeping agreements.

One of your functions is to help clarify expectations and agreements, not only between yourself and others, but among staff members. How can you do this?

• *An atmosphere of trust needs to be established within the staff.* If it does not exist, people will make commitments because they want to placate others, or because of fear.

• *You must convey the need for clarity.* For example, "I'd like to make certain we know what each of us is going to do. This will help me to fulfill my part of the agreement. In addition, I'd like to know whether my understanding is the same as yours, so that later we don't run into trouble."

• *You need to paraphrase what you hear from others.* Make it clear that each person understands about the agreements. It is necessary to know what they are to do, by when they are expected to do it, and how you will know whether they've done it.

• *When agreements have been fulfilled, show your appreciation.* If part of an agreement has not been completed, call it to the person's attention, and emphasize the importance of getting it done. For example: "Mr. Jones, it was my understanding at our meeting last week that you would have the report ready today. I feel bad that it isn't done, since it holds up our progress."

• *If an agreement has not been fulfilled, discuss the blocks to completing it.* When these are discussed in a problem-solving atmosphere, it reduces the need for rationalization and excuses.

• *Let there be an explicit understanding that if people cannot fulfill their agreement, they should immediately notify the others involved.* This recognizes that changing circumstances do occur, which sometimes make it difficult to fulfill agreements. Let there also be an agreement about how agreements can be changed.

4.25 Translating Blame Into Problem Solving

When people blame each other, it escalates conflict. Why is this so common?

• We all try to avoid feeling "wrong." Often we feel "right" by making the other person "wrong." The label of "being wrong" has such tremendous emotional implications that we will fight to avoid carrying that burden. We label each other as being right or wrong rather than seeing that—

1. Agreements have not been made clear.
2. Someone has not kept an agreement.
3. Someone made an assumption that turned out to be inaccurate.
4. Something did not happen as people expected it would.

• We feel that to admit a mistake or poor judgment is often a sign of weakness. However, we all make inaccurate judgments, we all experience unmet expectations, and we all have been in circumstances where agreements have not been made clear. Moreover, we all have avoided carrying through on some responsibilities because of the onerous work involved.

It is necessary to change blame into problem solving. The question is not who is to blame, but what can we do to change the situation and improve it. Here are the steps you can take:

• *People should be encouraged to state their feelings–and, moreover, these feelings should be listened to.* For example: "How do you feel about _____ ?" I sense that you are really angry at me for what I've done. Is that so?"

• *Seek information about what you or someone else is doing that disturbs others.* For example: "Could you tell me in a little more detail exactly what I did so I can understand my own behavior better?" "Could you let me know more about what I did that upset you?" By being assertive, and asking for negative feedback, you can frequently reduce the anger in other people's criticism.

• *If there is some validity in what the other person is accusing you of, admit it.* For instance, "It is possible that I came down on the faculty too hard, and I ignored some of the positive things they did." It is important, when you've admitted the validity of what the other person said, that you don't add, "But . . ." "But . . ." is often designed to negate or reduce the validity of what has just been said.

• *Make statements that the relationship is important to you and you'd like to work out the problem.* "I feel it is important that the anger we're feeling does not stand between you and me, and I'd like to try to work it out."

• *Invite the other person to participate in problem solving and looking at alternatives.* For example: "Would you like to look at ways that we can change the situation? Maybe we could start by clarifying how we each see the problem."

4.3 COMMON CONFLICTS AND SUGGESTED APPROACHES TO RESOLVE THEM

The following are actual situations that have been faced by administrators in a number of schools. They are written so that you can test yourself. First read the case study, and then ask yourself, "How would I handle this?" In each *Analysis* we will list the features that need to be considered.

4.31   Case Study—Parent and Teacher Fight Over a Child

You have recently received a phone call from Mrs. S., who is unhappy about the way the third grade teacher, Mrs. Q., is handling her son, Joey. She stated that a number of parents are dissatisfied with Mrs. Q.'s handling of their children, and hinted that she would like Joey moved to another classroom.

You respect Mrs. Q. because of her sensitivity to children's needs. She maintains an informal, but productive, classroom. Mrs. Q. informed you that she sent a note to Mrs. S. about Joey talking too much in class. You know that the S. family, which has high standards, is not used to getting negative reports about their children.

Mrs. S. informed you that Joey has said that he tried hard to behave in school, but the other children bother him. On the other hand, Mrs. Q. has said that Joey complains that his parents put too much pressure on him to act properly.

4.311   Analysis

The parent and the teacher differ in their expectations about Joey's behavior, and have not been able to meet face to face in order to clarify and explore the differences. Moreover, neither seems to be aware that Joey is giving different stories at home and school. But, since both seem to trust you, you're in a good position to facilitate this meeting. It is important to remember that both the teacher's and the parent's competency and values are being threatened.

4.312   Suggested techniques for resolving

    a. Facilitate a meeting between parent and teacher (see Section 7.6).
    b. Suggest teacher send positive notes home, not just problems.
    c. Move toward agreement on Joey's responsibility in classroom.
    d. Clarify discrepancy in Joey's reports.
    e. Set limit regarding moving Joey; attempt to resolve problem within classroom.

4.32   Case Study—A Number of Teachers Do Not Like the Principal

You are a principal in a kindergarten-through-eighth-grade elementary school, that has a staff of 26 professional teachers. This is your first year and you are having difficulties with some of the older teachers who have been at the school for some time. You have brought in several new programs to the school that break with tradition, but are important for children in this community.

The conflict centers around the problem of getting teachers to make decisions. A few younger teachers are enthusiastic about working with you. A larger group of teachers, who have been here for some time, want you to make the decisions. But it seems that when you do, they don't like the decisions.

The school tradition is to have as few meetings as possible. You have tried to use the staff meetings for discussions, problem solving, and decision making, but have become frustrated at staff resistance. So now you use staff meetings only to communicate information.

The teachers live far apart, which hinders informal get-togethers. Because of the age range and diversity of background, there are no large groups of teachers who share much in common.

4.321   Analysis

There is mutual confusion between you and the teachers about your respective roles. Certain norms have been created by the school's history, which hinder participatory problem solving. You are in conflict with these norms, but have not created adequate arenas for discussion. Moreover, the polarization of the staff is accentuated by the lack of commonly shared experiences.

4.322   Suggested techniques for resolving

   a. Take a survey of staff regarding school climate, problem perception, etc. (see Sections 5.2 and 2.2).
   b. Suggest creation of Advisory Group, to include representative teachers, to analyze discrepancies uncovered in survey (see Sections 1.224 and 3.4).
   c. Consider role clarification process (see Section 10.3).
   d. Meet with small groups of teachers to get more input about decisions (see Sections 4.4 and 9.3).

4.33   Case Study—Staff Cliques at War with Each Other

One of the continuing conflicts at your school is what to do with misbehaving children. Over the years, the positions of two subgroups on the staff have hardened, with little resolution. One group, mainly the primary teachers, feel that the staff needs more time to talk to children and to institute creative and interesting programs. The other group, mainly the intermediate teachers, feel that more agreement about discipline is required to control the children.

Generally, the intermediate teachers are conservative in their teaching and don't have the resources that are available to the primary teachers, i.e., aides, special funds, etc.

You support the position of the primary teachers and are committed to individualized instruction. You want to create more informal attitudes among the children and staff.

There is another group of teachers, some primary and some intermediate, who complain about having to sit through discussions about discipline. They continue to send children to the office when they cannot manage them, and yet are dissatisfied with your handling of these children.

4.331 Analysis

The discrepancy between the primary and intermediate teachers is partly based on the differing needs of children at those levels. The split is accentuated, however, by the unequal distribution of resources, and their lack of functional interaction. The absence of a unified approach to discipline increases the conflict between you and the teachers. No effective problem-solving arena has been created.

4.332 Suggested techniques for resolving

  a. Use procedure for creating discipline program (see Section 3.6).
  b. Survey intermediate teachers regarding their needs.
  c. Create more opportunity for cross-grade communication (see Sections 9.2 and 4.4).
  d. Initiate more all-school activities and programs (see Sections 6.4 and 6.5).

4.34 Case Study—Which Reading Curriculum to Adopt

You are an elementary school principal in a rural area. The board of education has usually taken a strong, decisive hand in the management of the district. Most of the decisions that affect school policies and programs are made at the board level or at the central office.

The reading scores in a number of schools are not satisfactory to many parents. The board has provided more resources for reading programs, and has asked each school to determine which reading program it prefers.

Your staff has talked to different text book companies. The programs tend to fall into two categories. The "reductionist" approach is rigorous about requiring that children have each and every basic skill. The "holistic" approach relates reading to the total curriculum and offers activities that stimulate the overall reading capability in children.

It is clear to you and your staff that the central office is very concerned that each school be accountable for improving the reading scores of its children. You have heard that the administrators in the central office favor one of the reductionist programs. Most of your staff, who have lived in the community for some time, are afraid to make a decision that is not acceptable to the board and central office, though they are very interested in one of the holistic programs.

4.341 Analysis

The staff is confused about its decision-making powers in light of the history of the district, and because there has been no direct communication between them and the central office. You are not sure that you have the unanimous agreement of the staff, and thus, your role as staff advocate is shaky. Being caught in the middle can produce much stress.

4.342 Suggested techniques for resolving

   a. Invite central office administrator to meet with staff, regarding decision-making authority.
   b. Survey staff in order to get greater clarity about their preferences in reading programs.
   c. You need to clarify your position on reading program to staff.
   d. Staff needs to prepare their case for selection of program, possibly including parental support (see Sections 7.2 and 7.9).

4.35 Case Study—Two Teachers Don't Get Along

You have been the administrator for six years at an elementary school located in a suburban community. Generally speaking, your staff is competent, enthusiastic, and interested in what they're doing, and there is a good deal of parent support for the school.

At present, the staff is attempting to develop an integrated curriculum that will provide continuity through the primary and intermediate grades. Your teachers are working on developing curriculum components with each other, but one of the chronic problems of the school continues to interfere with this task. This problem is the traditional conflict between Mrs. A., who is a third grade teacher, and Miss D., who is a fourth grade teacher. These two have not been able to like or get along with each other.

In the past this has been tolerable, but now their conflicts have interfered with the development of the integrated curriculum project. Mrs. A. is a very good teacher who tends to be loud, boisterous, and frequently dominating. She has a great deal of confidence in her capabilities as a teacher. Miss D., a teacher of many years, is quiet and thoughtful, although, when attacked or criticized, she becomes sarcastic and defensive. She seems to lack confidence in spite of her long years of teaching.

The two teachers, up to now, have been able to avoid each other and do not engage in a great deal of backbiting or gossip about each other. The staff has tended to accept their relationship for what it is. But now, their relationship has bogged the project down.

4.351 Analysis

Each of the two teachers has differing needs which have not been fully recognized or respected. When everyone avoids the problem, these needs cannot be met. You have probably been avoiding taking on Mrs. A. because of her style, and have found it difficult to be honest with Miss D. because of her defensiveness.

4.352 Suggested techniques for resolving

a. Administrator needs to talk with each teacher about personal needs, her view of the conflict, and importance of resolving it (see Sections 8.6 and 4.4).
b. Administrator must clarify consequences of not resolving problem, including the effect on the project, transfer or replacement, and time demands.
c. Facilitate a face-to-face meeting between the teachers (see Section 8.6).
d. If two teachers don't work it out, administrator should publicly address problem to project staff.

4.36 Case Study—Some Staff Resistant to New Ideas

You recently attended an administrative seminar devoted to improving management skills and identifying problems that exist within a school. As a result of your experiences, you have become aware that the quality of communication within your school is not what it should be. Because of the multiplicity of federal programs, teachers are involved in a variety of activities and often get confused, frustrated and rushed.

At a staff meeting, you discussed this problem and the need for improving communication skills and procedures. While there is general agreement about the need, a number of the staff do not wish to take any more time in inservice training. They feel that it would take time away from required tasks. Others of the staff are very interested in acquiring these new skills. It is your opinion that the staff would have to move ahead as a whole.

4.361 Analysis

In a situation of high work pressure, communications easily break down, but often communicating effectively increases the work pressure. Your staff is not clear about who is responsible for communications, and you don't seem to have done everything you can. The uncertainty about how much self-disclosure will be involved in a communication workshop adds to staff resistance. Many of the teachers do not "own" the problem, since the initiative came from you.

4.362 Suggested techniques for resolving

    a. Survey staff on all features of communication problem (see Section 9.2).
    b. Survey staff about inservice training needs (see Section 1.221).
    c. Create a subcommittee of those teachers interested in the issue.
    d. Make brief communication workshop voluntary (see Chapter 9).
    e. Clarify administrator's communication responsibilities and unilaterally insure that they're done.

4.37 Case Study—Principal Not Getting Along with Central Office

There is a new superintendent of schools in your district, who has brought with him a number of experienced administrators. He wishes to review district procedures and create a team-oriented administrative structure in line with new board policy. The changes involve both central office administrators and building administrators like yourself.

Your district is quite spread out geographically, and your school is at the fringes of the district. It therefore takes a long time for you to drive from your school to the central office and back. Meetings to plan and discuss this new administrative structure are often called at the last minute, and last a long time. A number of teachers are very unhappy about your being away from school so much. You have sensed that others are also resentful but are not speaking up. You have always prided yourself on being available to parents and teachers. You can understand and appreciate the new superintendent's purpose, but nevertheless are quite resentful about the amount of time that you are required to be away from school.

4.371 Analysis

Central office does not understand your position, and apparently you have not communicated it directly. It also seems that your teachers are unaware of the pressure on you. The new superintendent really needs to know what goes on in your school. It's hard to challenge central office.

4.372 Suggested techniques for resolving

    a. Administrator raise problem in "team" meeting to determine whether others experience the same problem (see Section 8.5).
    b. Meet with staff to discuss their needs and your problem.

    c. Create small committee to define procedures while principal is absent.

    d. Administrator should consider setting limit on time devoted to project (see Chapter 8).

4.4 HOW TO CREATE A CLIMATE TO LESSEN THE FREQUENCY AND SEVERITY OF CONFLICTS

By creating a proper school atmosphere, you can markedly reduce the severity and frequency of conflict. As administrator you can do much to foster the attitude that conflicts are occasions for problem solving; that facing disagreements can create energy, but avoiding them results in low morale and loss of energy.

4.41 Establish Forums for Expression of Grievances

In order to work at reducing conflict, there have to be occasions at which discussion can occur. This section evaluates various forums.

4.411 Staff meetings

The administrator needs to be aware of both the advantages and disadvantages of using the staff meeting as a place to resolve conflict. The following are advantages that staff meetings offer in working through *certain kinds* of conflicts:

1. The whole staff can provide a broad range of input on school-wide problems.

2. The problems identified can be referred to subcommittees consisting of people who are truly interested in a particular problem. Those who are not interested need not wade through meetings about problems unrelated to them.

3. When the total staff sees how conflicts can be changed into problem-solving procedures, a climate can be encouraged where conflicts are openly dealt with.

However, there are certain disadvantages that the administrator needs to be aware of:

1. In most staff meetings, infrequently held, a tight agenda under time constraints precludes thoughtful consideration of problems.

2. Unless subgroups are used effectively, people who are uninvolved in a problem become frustrated by hearing about it.

3. Some people are hesitant to speak up in large groups.

4. Large groups try to find solutions too quickly, not giving enough time to defining and analyzing the problem.

If you use staff meetings to solve problems, you need to know how to use small groups, and appropriate problem-solving steps.

4.412   Administrator-teacher conferences

Many conflicts are limited to two people, and require you to work with one or two teachers. The advantage of such meetings is that if trust exists between you and the teachers, they have a narrower focus and people feel freer to disclose the sources of the conflict. Successful outcomes in these meetings reinforce good relationships between you and the teacher.

The following are ways to increase the effectiveness of such meetings:

1. Meet on a neutral ground when possible. Teachers often feel intimidated by being "called on the carpet."

2. It is important that you and individual teachers get together periodically to discuss positive aspects of the teacher's behavior. Avoid the appearance that conferences only deal with problems.

3. When conducting the meeting, you must really listen to what the teachers say and make sure that their feelings are expressed; and you need to indicate where you stand and not leave ambiguity about your view of the meeting.

4. If trust is high, get permission to record the meeting. This allows a more thoughtful review of the main points.

5. It is supportive if the teachers know that you are trying to identify the things they need in order to do a better job. They must know that you can help them to meet these needs.

6. Be careful about making promises that you cannot fulfill, and avoid raising the teachers' expectations unrealistically.

4.413   Grade level meetings

Grade level meetings are where teachers of the same or closely related grades, i.e., primary or intermediate, discuss problems of common interest. At these meetings teachers who share similar responsibilities can share resources. Furthermore, if some teachers are concerned about an issue, they can check out their perceptions with those who are in a similar position. Teachers who are feeling angry and resentful often need the support of others on the staff, in order to voice these frustrations in a larger context.

Your role is to encourage such meetings and to provide expertise in facilitating the process.

4.414   Interest groups

Interest groups are those in which people with similar interests meet for limited purposes. These groups have a narrow focus, such as generating a program, getting information, developing a solution to a problem, etc.

The advantage of this grouping is that people who are highly interested in a topic take more responsibility and have more commitment than those who are not. If the school encourages such groups to form, then people feel that they will be able to share common concerns in a supportive problem-solving group.

Here's how you can help make such groups effective:

1. You should help the group define its purpose, membership, and responsibility to the larger staff.

2. You can insure that membership in these groups is voluntary.

3. You can help the group limit its responsibility and clarify the relationship between it and the larger staff. Interest groups should always be subordinate to other decision-making bodies within the school.

4.415   Teams

Teams are groups of two to four, who work closely together frequently and over a significant period of time. Teams, as distinct from interest groups, often deal with more general and ongoing issues within the school. An interest group may be created to plan a Christmas party, but a team might be involved in text book review. Teams may deal with issues because of obligation rather than interest. However, if properly conducted they can reinforce the idea of sharing in such responsibilities as part of a cohesive staff.

One advantage of a team is that people can acquire considerable expertise in an area by having to deal with it over a long period of time.

Here's how you can increase the effectiveness of such groups:

1. You can assist the members to define their roles on the team. The group functions very much as any team does, i.e., individual skills and interests should be considered in assigning responsibilities.

2. You can encourage the group to talk about its own procedures when interest flags and people become uninvolved. Such a discussion can renew interest and ventilate frustrated feelings.

3. You can encourage clarification of the purpose and responsibilities of the team.

4.42   Administrator as a Model

Due to your position and the fact that you coordinate the activities of many people, your influence on the school is both intensive and pervasive. This role forces you to be a model for staff and students.

You serve as a model in a number of different ways:

1. Your staff watches closely the manner in which you tackle conflict, and take their cues from you.

2. When you can change blame into problem solving, listen effectively, and state your opinion clearly, it makes it much easier for the staff to do likewise.

3. By serving as an effective facilitator, you model good communication and problem-solving skills which can be emulated by the staff.

4. When *you* handle criticism well, your staff will be less defensive.

5. When you are vague, non-commital, and distant, the anxiety that is created will encourage your staff to respond similarly.

4.43   Use Natural Leadership in the Staff

You are not alone with the conflict. There are many natural leaders and problem solvers on your staff. Some people are good at leading meetings, while others are wonderful at resolving conflicts between two or more people. People can be encouraged by you to mediate conflicts and take leadership in group problem solving. You, however, must guard against biases in selecting leaders and should honestly consider the capabilities and aptitudes of those whose point of view differs from yours. Moreover, you should avoid expecting too much from any one person. The staff person who is an excellent facilitator for small group discussion may freeze up when facing a large group. Using the natural leadership within the staff is an extension of your own leadership role.

At one school the administrator divided the faculty into problem-solving teams. After a period of training, he attended team meetings infrequently. The team leaders formed an Administrative Council, to which each team reported. The morale of the staff was high, and all teachers were involved.

4.44   Make Disagreement a Virtue, Rather Than a Problem

By seeking alternative viewpoints, you create a climate in which the expression of differences becomes a virtue rather than a problem. How can this be done?

1. You can play the "devil's advocate," after making clear that you are doing so. But you must avoid hiding behind criticism rather than stating your opinion clearly.

2. You can make it clear that by selecting people of differing viewpoints to work together you intend to encourage creative solutions.

3. When leading a meeting you can seek differing points of view, and encourage expression of these differences.

4.45   Informal Methods

In any social system, the more opportunities that people have to relate to each other, the more likely it is that they will be flexible in solving conflicts. The degree to which people know each other in different ways determines how tolerant they are of each other's idiosyncracies. You should encourage the development of activities that are not strictly related to the work of the school. Parties, fairs, faculty-student contests, races, etc., are examples. At one school, where faculty was relatively uninvolved in meetings and problem solving, the principal initiated a "Contest Day" between students and faculty. She came dressed as a clown and distributed prizes to faculty and children. The faculty was able to laugh at her and at each other. In this spirit, many problems that seemed insurmountable were faced and worked through. You should also try to devote time periodically at staff meetings to creative ideas rather than heavy problem solving. Humor is a magic potion that you can use in resolving conflicts.

It's important that informal methods arise from the interests of the staff. You can, however, initiate discussions and encourage exploration of a wide range of activities. Many such ideas will be good for children as well as staff.

4.5 HOW TO USE QUESTIONNAIRES AND SURVEYS TO HEAD OFF OR REDUCE CONFLICTS

Questionnaires and surveys can be effective tools in gathering information quickly and objectively. Moreover, people can more readily accept objective data than information verbally given by the people with whom they are in conflict.

4.51 When to Use

The following are criteria that you can use to determine the usefulness of questionnaires:

• When there is high conflict and feelings are intense, a survey can assure anonymity and allow the expression of underlying feelings.

• A questionnaire can objectively compare how different segments of a staff and community feel about a particular issue. It can thus be determined to what extent differences of viewpoint are sources of conflict.

• Questionnaires can provide ongoing evaluation of a new program or procedure, e.g., parent newsletter, so that corrective action can be quickly taken.

• A survey can verify the extent to which a rumor is true and thus head off future conflict.

• You can use a survey when pressured by a segment of parents in order to determine how representative these parents' views are.

5

How to Improve
School Climate

If you have been around schools for some time, you may be able to sense the climate of a school almost as soon as you enter it. If you remain at a school for some time, becoming part of the system of human relationships and day-to-day activities, the "sense" referred to above often dissipates.

In recent years, studies have attempted to clarify the factors involved in school climate. Section 1.3 of this Handbook describes ways to measure the quality of the climate in your school.

School climate is perceived and reacted to by the people within your school. People don't often think about it analytically, but it influences everyone's behavior. It's the summation of people's feelings about the way certain things happen at your school:

- The degree to which people feel comfortable when at the school.
- Whether everyone performs his assigned tasks satisfactorily.
- The degree to which interpersonal relations at the school are productive and satisfying.
- Whether people tend to reach agreement easily, and resolve conflicts quickly.
- If rules and regulations are upheld and obeyed.

All of these issues are determined by the norms of behavior that exist at your school. These group norms, or shared expectations, sometimes only dimly perceived, are the building blocks of school climate.

5.1 EVALUATING THE SCHOOL CLIMATE

This chapter and Section 1.3 provide a framework for understanding and measuring school climate. Chapter 6, on Self-Esteem, contains useful information about things you can do to improve school climate.

5.2 CHANGING GROUP NORMS AS THE BASIS FOR CHANGING THE SCHOOL CLIMATE

What people believe determines how they act. This section will show you how to evaluate and effect changes in beliefs at your school.

5.21 What Is a Group Norm?

A group norm is the "idea" about how it is appropriate to act in a specific situation, which is shared by the members of a group. This "idea" affects how people expect themselves and others to act, and determines their attitudes about such behavior.

Group norms differ in the degree of intensity that people feel about them. People would be much more upset if conflicts were resolved in your staff by physical violence, than if someone forgets to wash her coffee cup.

Some norms have narrow limits; others are more flexible. The expectation that teachers will be in their classes when school begins is an example of a norm that allows for little variation. Whether or not teachers leave their rooms during recesses can be handled differently by different teachers. Norms that have narrow limits have the force of a rule, and often become so.

There are two major dimensions by which norms influence school climate. These are:

a. The *degree of importance* with which people invest the area in which the norm exists.
b. The *degree of consensus* that exists in the group about the norm.

The *degree of importance* reflects the judgment that the group makes that some particular area of behavior, e.g., being on time to meetings, is critical to the performance and well-being of the group.

The *degree of consensus* is a measure of (1) what proportion of a group agrees that a norm is important, and (2) the variability that is permitted in carrying out the norm.

Figure 5-1 shows how this can be made graphic.

	Degree of Consensus	
	Lo Consensus	Hi Consensus
Unimportant	Many individual differences will be tolerated. Most will not be critical of how others act. Little disagreement or conflict will arise. People will be free to "do their own thing" in their own way. Norms such as these do not contribute to group cohesion.	People are very like each other, and anyone who is very different will have a hard time in the group. The group may tend toward rigidity, and change is not easy to bring about. Most people will feel comfortable, except those who don't share in the consensus, who will be seen as "tolerated deviants."
Very Important	Disagreement and conflict will arise around these norms. People will tend to be critical of others. Cliques can form. Agreement about performance and expectations will be low. There has probably been little productive discussion about these norms.	Clarity about expectations is high, so there is little need to talk about these norms very much. People understand what they are to do, and what others will do. These norms contribute to the productivity of the group. When people act in accordance with these norms, they experience great satisfaction and approval. When they don't, the social and interpersonal penalties are severe.

Degree of Importance (left axis label)

FIGURE 5-1

Here are some examples of the above categories:

a. Lo Consensus/Unimportant
   What teachers wear to school is not instrumental in producing learning, and teachers wear what they wish.
      (Norms about what clothing is appropriate to wear to school.)

Check these over! (handwritten annotation)

b. Lo Consensus/Important
   When a staff feels strongly that the school has a problem in discipline, but can't agree on how to handle it.
   (Norms about how to handle children who misbehave.)
c. Hi Consensus/Unimportant
   When most staff enjoy eating together in the teacher's room, but some prefer eating in the classrooms.
   (Norms about social interaction among staff.)
d. Hi Consensus/Very Important
   When all teachers spend considerable time managing their classes in such a way as to keep rowdiness and excessive noise to a minimum.
   (Norms about professional behavior.)

Group norms exist in all areas of a school's activities. There is little that people do that is not influenced by such norms. Figure 5-2 shows the areas in which norms exist, and examples of norms that may exist in each area. Use this as a preliminary checklist, and see which norms are exemplified in the behavior of your staff.

A. Norms about behavior in meetings:
   • People should pay close attention to the speaker.
   • It's O.K. to correct papers or knit during meetings.
   • Everyone should be prompt to meetings.
   • If someone has something important to say, he can interrupt another.
   • There should be a chairperson at all meetings.
   • Meetings should be "serious," not "light."
B. Norms about decision making:
   • Teachers cannot influence decisions.
   • Group consensus is important in major decisions.
   • The administrator should only make those decisions that no one else wants to make.
   • If a minority doesn't agree to a decision, it's just "tough."
   • People should be able to decide things for themselves.
C. Norms about how the school is thought of:
   • This is a great school, and most things that happen here are good.
   • This is a bad school, and we're lucky when something good happens.
   • There's nothing very special about this school.
   • This is a school with a lot of strange people in it.
   • The dignity of this school should be preserved.
   • This school needs to be protected from its critics.
D. Norms about taking responsibility:
   • It's best not to volunteer too much.

FIGURE 5-2

- Anyone who feels responsible should be responsible.
- It's important that responsibilities are shared equally.
- Everyone should put in more time than expected.
- Don't do more than you're paid for.

E. Norms about standards:
- Don't expect too much, or else you'll be disappointed.
- Everyone should strive toward excellence.
- There's nothing wrong with being average.
- There are some people who just can't do very well.
- Expect the best; get the best.

F. Norms about differences:
- It's not good to be different.
- Being different is a problem.
- Diversity is exciting.
- People who are different are interesting.
- Differences mean disagreements and fights.
- Differences between people are stimulating.

G. Norms about authority:
- Don't rock the boat.
- People above you know best.
- Those in authority should not be trusted.
- People in authority will take care of us.
- No one should be able to tell anyone else what to do.
- Authority should be respected only when it's handled well.

H. Norms about interpersonal relationships:
- Everyone should be part of the group.
- People who work together don't have to be friends outside of school.
- You can't expect everyone to get along with each other.
- It's all right if a few people are not part of the group.
- People should be left alone to "do their own thing."
- People should be encouraged to feel part of the group.

I. Norms about parent involvement in the school:
- Having parents around is more trouble than it's worth.
- Parent involvement helps teachers do a better job.
- Only snoopy parents want to be involved in the school.
- Parent involvement shows they don't trust us.
- It's fun having parents around.

J. Norms about innovation and change:
- It's best not to change things too much.
- Change indicates growth and vitality.
- If change disturbs anyone, it should be avoided.
- Things aren't likely to change much around here.
- Everything can be improved.
- Trying to change things leads to problems.

FIGURE 5-2 *(continued)*

K. Norms about children's behavior:
  • Give them an inch; they'll take a mile.
  • Kids are basically good; they just make mistakes.
  • If you love a child enough, he'll turn out all right.
  • Kids need to be trained to act correctly.
  • You can't expect too much, or some kids will fail.
  • You get what you expect from kids.

FIGURE 5-2 (continued)

5.211 How to identify it

There are two ways to identify a group norm. One is to observe what people do; the other is to ask what they believe. As a school administrator you may have little inclination and no time to pursue an abstract investigation of the group norms within your staff or school. There are occasions, though, when it would be useful to understand what norms you are dealing with.

These occasions are those in which your purposes seem to be impeded by staff lethargy, unwillingness to change, or chronic repetition of old problems. These are indicators that some dysfunctional group norms are operative.

In the bibliography there are references to survey instruments that are designed to identify the norms a group holds. These will give you guides to constructing questionnaires that can help you identify norms by asking people what they believe. Other chapters in this Handbook suggest survey/questionnaire techniques that will also assist you in uncovering the attitudes your staff holds.

One of the most important functions you can perform is as *observer* of the processes within your staff. In effect, you are always trying to make sense out of the ways in which you see your staff perform. Norms, which are the basis of group behavior, determine the ways in which your staff functions. When you see a pattern of behavior repeat itself many times, you are observing a norm.

Being an observer requires that you be in situations that allow you to observe. Being an active participant can interfere with being an objective observer. Your role as administrator in the school will allow you to be somewhat objective, although it is important to be aware that staff will show you behavior they want you to see. Any degree of objectivity provides an advantage in determining group norms.

Your ability to observe staff is helped by your being where they are:

  • Be with your staff in the teachers' lounge during breaks, recesses and lunches.
  • Visit classrooms often and regularly.
  • Organize staff meetings so that others are responsible for conducting them from time to time, so that you can relax and watch staff behavior.

- Participate in inservice programs with the staff.
- Meet with small groups of teachers periodically in order to find out what's going on.
- Be on the playground during recesses as often as possible.

5.212 How to clarify it

The clarification of group norms must occur within the group that holds the norm. The vehicle for doing this is communication.

Many other sections of the Handbook describe methods for holding effective group discussions.

The virtue of discussing group norms is having the group become self-conscious about how it operates. When a group becomes more aware of the bases of its own behavior, it can have more influence and control over its own purposes and goals.

An athletic team, in order to be successful, must continually assess its resources, evaluate the strengths and weaknesses of its members, plan strategies that maximize its strengths and minimize the effect of its weaknesses, and improve its attitude through commonly shared perceptions. Likewise, the staff of a school, when employing the same approach, can raise its collective performance and improve the climate of the school. Group norms, depending on what they are, contribute to the success or failure of the team.

5.213 How to change it

There are important issues to keep in mind when you consider changing group norms.

- Norms always are expressed in the behavior of the group. Changing a norm means changing the way people act. When the members of a group decide to act in new ways, there must be clarity and consensus about the new behavior, and reinforcement for it.
- It takes time to change the way a group behaves. Planning and patience are required by all, until a new behavior/norm is established.
- A new norm must satisfy some need of the group and its members better than the old norm, or else people will have little motivation to change. An example of this occurred in Cedar Elementary School. The administrator was new, having come from outside the district, and was unfamiliar with the conditions at Cedar. One of the chronic problem areas at the school was the lunchroom, where hot meals were cooked and served. Noisy, disruptive behavior had made it necessary to have several teachers police lunches, and the staff had become resigned to handling lunchroom behavior with a heavy hand. No one seemed to have any ideas about how to change things.

The administrator, Wayne Bannion, disturbed by the attitudes of both staff and students in the lunchroom arranged some teacher meetings during one lunch period, offering to monitor lunch himself that day. The teachers thought he was foolhardy, but were happy to be excused from duty. Bannion arranged to have the school's P.A. system placed in the cafeteria, and when the children sat down, he called for their attention, and said, "I'm all alone with you people today, and really need your help so that things don't get out of hand. I'd like to ask you to keep the noise down and control yourselves. I can promise you this: if lunch goes all right, you will be pleasantly surprised by what you'll get after lunch." In addition to that, he made a few comments about Cedar, cracked a few jokes, had all the children laughing—and lunch was very peaceful.

After lunch, a special ice-cream dessert was served, and the children had an extended recess so that teachers could finish their meetings. For the next few days, Bannion came to the lunchroom with the regular lunch-duty teachers. He talked to the children over the P.A. system each time, and encouraged the teachers to eat with the children, rather than patrol the aisles. The climate of the lunchroom improved and remained stable. A new norm was becoming established—that lunch could be a happy, relaxed time. Other positive reinforcers were introduced, such as special desserts, funny announcements, and the like.

• When new behavior occurs, positive reinforcement, often in the form of appropriate feedback, should happen. New norms need such reinforcement, both to give people a reward for changing, and to keep them aware of the issue.

• As an administrator, you have power to affect norms. You will do so more often through positive example than through authoritative fiat. Doing so may initially serve to make you feel somewhat isolated from the staff, but will have a strong positive influence on others' attitudes.

5.22 Agreement on Norms as the Basis for Improving Climate

There is no one "best" way for a school to be, but there are several characteristics that good schools share:

• A low degree of intra-staff conflict.
• A high degree of agreement on goals.
• A high degree of clarity about roles and functions.
• A positive climate, with a high degree of productivity.

Agreement about norms within a school means that a staff shares common perceptions about the way things are, the way they would like things to be, and the process for getting from one to the other.

To the extent that norms are identified, clarified through discussion, and changed through staff consensus, a feeling of participation in a common effort will be widespread through the staff.

At the beginning of this chapter (see page 121), we listed several of the characteristics that make up school climate. The norms or standards by which people behave, determine how these climate factors will be experienced. When the members of a group tend toward agreement about norms of behavior, and are *aware* that these agreements *are* shared by others, comfort, security, productivity, and cooperation increase. Without such awareness and agreement, cliques will form, blaming will occur, conflicts will be unresolved, and morale will decline.

5.23   Satisfaction and Productivity as Criteria of Positive Climate

There are two major issues that influence the degree to which an organization will have a positive climate. These are:

a. The extent to which the personal needs of the members of the group are satisfied by being a part of the group.
b. Whether the group is being productive in meeting its goals and objectives, and each member shares the feeling of productivity.

The two issues will be discussed in greater detail below.

5.231   Satisfaction is mainly related to personal needs and group relations

(Refer to Chapter 6, on Self-Esteem, especially the four conditions necessary for high self-esteem.) Human beings, being social animals, depend on the groups to which they belong for the satisfaction of basic human needs. On a large scale, our membership in the economic system of our community and nation insures that we will have food, power, water, and other essentials, which satisfy our biological needs. Families, work groups, friendship groups, clubs, teams, and other groups to which we belong, when taken together, must satisfy our needs for affiliation, security, influence, curiosity, achievement—and all the personal needs that human beings have.

Your school is a human group, which can partially fulfill a broad range of personal and social needs of its members. Insofar as it does that, the members of your staff will have positive feelings about being part of it, and will perceive their experience in the school in a positive light. These positive feelings and perceptions are the essential ingredients of a good climate.

It is, of course, unrealistic to assume that the school can satisfy even a major part of all the needs of staff, except those that are related to work or vocation. But in this area there are some important needs that can be satisfied by applying the principles and procedures that are illuminated in this Handbook. Among these are:

- the need to be protected from excessive conflict.
- the need to be heard, and well thought of by associates.
- the need to express talents and competencies and gain the appreciation of others for them.
- the need to share personal and important aspects of one's life with a person who shows warmth and caring.
- the need to understand and work within rules and limits.
- the need to control the condition of one's life.

However such human needs are stated, it is clear that if the situation at your school is one that frustrates these needs, the dissatisfactions that occur will result in a poor climate.

5.232   Productivity is related to staff's ability to meet clear standards, agreed to by the group

Productivity contributes to the satisfaction of personal needs.

It is also a discriminable factor that needs to be considered apart from personal needs.

Productivity in a school setting is an ambiguous factor. Educators constantly attempt to make it precise and measurable. The approach we take in the Handbook is more simple than most.

A *sense* of productivity, apart from standard measures of student achievement, is attainable when a school meets its goals and objectives. To the extent that such goals and objectives have arisen from the interests and purposes of the members of the group, the staff will feel ownership of and responsibility for them.

A school in which these factors are unclear, or in which goals are not agreed to by the staff, will experience ambiguity, confusion, and frustration when trying to determine how productive it is. The sense, by a group, that it is being productive, in its own terms, serves to improve the school climate.

Thus, productivity has two elements. One is the actual output of energy and time that the members of the group expend. The second is the degree to which the group can measure its performance against some standard it has agreed to. ''Are we doing better or worse?'' ''Are we doing more or less?'' Unless the group, and its members, have some clear guidelines for answering these questions, it will not be able either to sense or to measure its own productivity. In such an environment, the work climate of the school will deteriorate.

6

Developing Greater Self-Esteem

This chapter shows how self-esteem influences all the things that happen in your school. The ideas presented here will help you and your staff to improve your interactions with each other and with children, and will improve the total self-esteem climate in the school.

6.1   WHAT IS SELF-ESTEEM?

Self-esteem is not a mystery. In our day-to-day interaction with people we often sense whether or not a person has high or low self-esteem. We do so by making judgments based on our observations of a person's behavior, and how we interpret them. Figure 6-1 points out some of the indexes of high and low self-esteem.

6.11   What is the Difference Between Self-Concept and Self-Esteem?

Self-concept has been identified as "a theory that an individual has unwittingly constructed about himself as an experiencing, functioning individual. . . ."[1]

As a "theory," self-concept is basically a set of ideas that a person holds about himself, some of which may be accurate, and others inaccurate.

---

[1]Epstein, Seymour, "The Self-Concept Revisited," *American Psychologist*, May 1973, pp. 404 to 416.

Characteristics of persons with high self-esteem:

Feel worthwhile.

Willing to take risks.

Confident about values and
  beliefs.

Set clear limits for self and
  others.

Can be objective and dispas-
  sionate.

Approach new challenges with
  enthusiasm.

Feel capable of exerting
  influence.

Proud of accomplishments.

Can act independently.

Have faith in the future.

Make accurate judgments
  about themselves.

Assume responsibility easily.

Tolerate frustration well.

Characteristics of persons with low self-esteem:

Feel unworthy.

Feel powerless.

Unsure or ambivalent about
  beliefs.

Easily influenced by others.

Confused about own reality.

Feel that others don't value them.

Blame others for own faults or
  weaknesses.

Avoid situations that pro-
  voke anxiety.

Demean own talents.

Often need emotional support.

Pessimistic about the future.

Cannot control own emotions.

Approach new situations with
  caution.

Become defensive when
  frustrated.

FIGURE 6-1

Self-esteem is related to self-concept in that it is a sense of satisfaction that a person experiences when he feels that:

- He has adequately expressed his self-concept in performance.
- He has fulfilled the personal standards associated with his self-concept.
- He has had his self-concept confirmed by others.

Self-concept can be reported; self-esteem is experienced. Self-esteem is an unconscious, emotional reflection of one's judgment about self. Self-esteem is always expressed in a person's behavior.

6.12 Self-Esteem as a Motive to Behavior

There are several common motives that guide behavior. These motives *may* conflict with each other, resulting in stress for an individual and those around him.

1. A person will tend to behave so as to increase his sense of worth.
2. A person will tend to act so as to confirm his self-image.
3. A person will act so as to maintain a *constant* self-image, irrespective of changing circumstances.

6.2 HOW HIGH SELF-ESTEEM AFFECTS LEARNING AND HUMAN RELATIONS

Many studies of self-esteem have shown that it is an important factor in academic performance and human relations. A school administrator can benefit from a knowledge of this relationship.

6.21 Self-Esteem and Academic Performance

Purkey, in a review of research about self-concept and academic performance, points out that a strong reciprocal relationship exists between the two.[2] High self-esteem aids in learning, and performing well at school helps in increasing self-esteem.

Case Example: Lonnie was a very bright, underachieving third grade boy, the son of two school teachers. His academic performance was far behind that of the rest of his class, and he often was the center of trouble in the classroom and on the playground. Rewards, punishments, parent conferences and other tactics were used to motivate him to work; all to no avail. He would only do a bit of work if the teacher hovered over him. Lonnie was interested in art, and complained about not being able to do it enough, although much time was allowed for it. His parents were most interested in his academic progress.

As a last-ditch effort, Lonnie's teacher decided to try an experiment. She told him that he could do art and craft work for as long as he wished, the only limitation being that if he wanted to stop, he either had to sit quietly in his seat or do some academic work. He could choose.

During the next two weeks, Lonnie did nothing but art work all day. (In an unstructured, open classroom, his special status didn't stand out.) During this time he created a puppet show for the first graders, and another for his classmates. He produced many other art projects, and, most significantly, was not a behavior problem. After almost two weeks, when the teacher was beginning to feel that her experiment was not producing the results she'd hoped for, Lonnie approached her saying that he was getting bored doing art work, and wished to return to academics. He rejoined the class willingly.

Lonnie's case represents two significant features of self-esteem: his sense

---

[2]Purkey, W. W. *Self Concept and School Achievement*, Prentice-Hall, 1970.

of *uniqueness*, with the resultant public approval of his special talent, and his sense of *power*, the ability to choose what he would do. His improved motivation in academics was a byproduct of his better feelings about himself.

6.22   Self-Esteem and Getting Along With Others

Coopersmith points out that children with high self-esteem usually have better interpersonal relationships and are often chosen for leadership positions. These children expect that they will be successful and influential in their relations with others.[3]

High self-esteem does not seem to result in attitudes of superiority. People with high self-esteem reflect the attitude of acceptance and respect which they have received and which is central to their own sense of self-worth.

Acceptance and respect are attitudes which you, as an administrator, can promote in your school. The impact on self-esteem can be significant for adults as well as for children.

6.23   Self-Esteem and Creativity

Creative expression is characterized by an ability to take risks and organize resources in a unique and personal manner. Being able to take risks is based, to a large extent, on feelings of self-assurance and competence. Persons with high self-esteem are self-assured, and demonstrate creativity more often in what they do. They reinforce positive feelings about themselves by gaining public approval with unique and outstanding productivity. People with low self-esteem fear to make mistakes that result in disapproval. They tend to be overly cautious.

Case Example: The staff at MacNeil School was unhappy with their performance, and felt that they needed to be more creative with children. With the help of consultants, they adopted a program to raise the self-esteem of the children in school by a measurable amount, based on pre- and post-testing. The decision to undertake the project was made by the staff and supported by the principal, who had traditionally been an authoritarian administrator. At first cautious and highly dependent on the consultants' guidance, the staff gradually gained enthusiasm and interest in the project. By means of small group exercises, team teaching, and a supportive attitude, the climate of the school was improved, and teachers began to initiate new programs.

During the year, many innovative programs were begun. By the end of the year, the teachers developed a handbook on raising self-esteem, which was used by other schools. The concept of teacher participation in decisions was firmly

---

[3]Coopersmith, S. *The Antecedents of Self-Esteem*, W. H. Freeman, 1967.

incorporated, and there was a significant increase in the measured self-esteem of the student body.

One of the more interesting features of the above case was that the staff of MacNeil school became increasingly self-conscious about their own self-esteem during the project, and did things that made their jobs more satisfying, such as having refreshments in the teachers' room, giving parties, and attempting minor innovations without the administrator's prior approval. They used each other as models for creative change, and incorporated self-esteem issues as a central element in their school's goals.

for mid-term!

6.3   THE FOUR INGREDIENTS OF SELF-ESTEEM

Certain conditions must be met for people to have a high sense of self-esteem. The conditions must be present *continuously* for a high sense of self-esteem to be maintained. Teachers and school administrators may not be able to control the reinforcement of these conditions at home, but can promote them in the school.

6.31   Connectiveness—The Importance of Relationships to People and Things

For high self-esteem, one must have the opportunity to gain satisfaction from valued associations, and the importance of these associations must be affirmed by others. In Section 6.6 of this chapter, specific activities that enhance connectiveness will be described.

6.311   Increasing the OPPORTUNITY to gain satisfaction from valued associations

Things which increase opportunities for relationships are:
  • *Frequent occasions for people to interact with each other*. The opportunity for people to form groups can be increased in classrooms, and the school as a whole.
  • *Variety in the content of these occasions*. Athletics, clubs, study groups, games, and a wide variety of group opportunities allow individual interests to find expression.
  • *Structured, formal events that are goal oriented*. Meetings, work groups, committees, clean-up crews and other activities that involve structure, role clarity, clear goals, and a final product assist people to work together.
  • *Frequent informal events*. Parties, game times, hanging around,

spontaneity—all contribute to people's enjoyment of each other and the experiences they share.

• *An atmosphere that supports a sense of personal safety and security.* If people feel threatened, physically or psychologically, they will tend to avoid interacting with others.

• *Clarity about standards and limits in relationships.* When there is too much ambiguity about *how* people are to relate, anxiety will keep them separate from each other.

6.312   How to GAIN SATISFACTION from valued associations

You have no doubt sensed the satisfying feeling that results from a successful interaction with another person. Conversely, when we have a dissatisfying encounter, we generally experience a sense of loss, or frustration with ourselves.

We most often gain satisfaction from a relationship when:

• We have successfully reached some goal in the interaction.
• Our feeling of personal worth has been affirmed by others.
• We have upheld our personal values or beliefs.
• We have been accepted and recognized as being important.
• Our sense of personal security has been increased by the relationship.

You, as an administrator, can help people to interact so as to increase their satisfaction. With children or teachers, it's important to improve a sense of connectiveness by:

• Helping people clarify their own goals.
• Affirming the inherent worth of others.
• Allowing people to interact in areas that are mutually important.
• Giving people recognition for performance.
• Creating a climate of tolerance for differences.
• Giving evidence of affection to others and permitting its expression.
• Helping people to feel that they belong.

6.313   How to increase the VALUE of your associations

Self-esteem is influenced in a positive direction only if a person gains satisfaction in *interactions that are important.* Not every success makes us feel good. If I'm very good at something that I think is commonplace or unimportant, my self-esteem will not be positively affected.

Some high-achieving children do not seem to reap any personal reward from success in academics. Their performance is not self-satisfying, and they may feel that other things are more important than academic achievement.

A person will not have a positive sense of self-worth if he is kept from associating with people he values, and doing things he considers important.

As teacher or administrator, it is only possible to foster a positive sense of connectiveness *if you know what is important to the people with whom you're working*. When you have such knowledge, you can promote, for others, experiences that they value.

You can get to know what people value by creating opportunities to foster connectiveness *in which you participate*.

Here is how self-esteem can be positively influenced:

- Facilitate communications so that people can discover who shares common interests with them.
- Allow people to work at things they feel are important.
- Ask people what is important to *them*, and help them find ways to act in those areas.
- Respect the important connections that people experience, such as race, ethnic background, family, social group, etc.

6.32 Uniqueness—The Appreciation of Special Talents or Skills

A person must acknowledge, respect, and express those characteristics that he feels are special or unique about himself. These characteristics must also receive affirmation from others.

Persons with high self-esteem feel that the *combination* of attributes that personify them is special, more than a singular outstanding characteristic.

6.321 Acknowledging uniqueness

There are several reasons why people with low self-esteem lack a sense of uniqueness:

- They have never been told that some talent or skill is special, because they haven't been among people who appreciate it.
- Limitations of background or experience held back its expression.
- Economic constraints reduce the opportunity to practice it.
- Their special quality was also evidenced by others, who received greater recognition.
- Being different is not valued in their situation.

In order for a person to acknowledge his uniqueness, it is important that:

- He is given a way to evaluate himself without feeling threatened.
- Others tell him what they think is special about him.
- He is helped to recognize that differences are an important part of self.

6.322   Respecting uniqueness

A person may sense that something about himself is special, but may not respect it, for some of the reasons stated in Section 6.321.

Self-respect for uniqueness is increased by having those qualities respected by others. In order for you to acknowledge and respect the unique qualities of students and teachers, you must be aware of what they believe is special about themselves.

If a person feels that something about himself is special, but can't gain others' respect for that quality, he will either:

a. Withhold expression of this quality, or
b. Excessively express it in order to try to gain respect for it.

This latter bid for respect is greatly evidenced in schools where the expression of uniqueness is limited. The child who repeats a punishable act obsessively is asking to be respected for uniqueness, as is the teacher who always tries to be "different."

A sense of uniqueness is very precious, and much disruptive behavior is unconsciously designed to gain affirmation for it. Unless this need is satisfied, the disruption may continue.

Case Example: Tommy, a fifth grader, had a reputation as a "bad kid" in his school, and was often in fights. Repeatedly criticized and punished for fighting, he nevertheless remained hostile and aggressive. His teacher finally tried praise, and told him how much she respected his prowess at fighting, even though it wasn't allowed at school. After a brief period of fighting, Tommy calmed down and exercised greater self-restraint. He got along very well with his teacher.

6.323   Expressing uniqueness

In order to express uniqueness comfortably, the following conditions must be present:

- Acceptance of individual differences must be a norm in the environment.
- Feedback about what others see as special about a person must be available.
- Encouragement to do something unique must be offered.
- Opportunities for connectiveness must be available.
- People need to see others expressing their own uniqueness, especially those in authority.

People will be more creative when their self-esteem is supported by their being able to express their uniqueness. Administrators who encourage such expression have vital, energetic, and imaginative staffs. Children benefit from the creativity and self-esteem of their teachers.

6.33 Power—Being Able to Influence the Circumstances of One's Life

A person must have the resources, opportunity, and capability to influence the circumstances of his life and work.

Being powerless creates low feelings of self-esteem. People who feel powerless lack energy, motivation, ability to assume responsibility, imagination; teachers who feel powerless can't teach well, administrators who feel powerless manage things poorly.

Having a sense of power is not the same thing as having absolute control of all situations. A clear and honest recognition of personal or situational constraints can contribute to a sense of power.

A person who has an adequate sense of power might say, "I'm doing all I can, under the circumstances, and am comfortable with the results of my efforts. I am making optimal use of the resources and capabilities at my command."

A person who feels powerless might say, "I am not able to do what I want, and am never satisfied with my efforts. Resources are kept from me, and I'm not capable of doing what is necessary."

The essential ingredient for having a sense of power is the ability to make choices and decisions and to carry them out. Severe constraints on this ability, whether personal or situational, will result in feelings of lack of power.

6.331 Making resources available

In a school, where power is usually a function of individual effort coordinated through group processes, other resources are required for personal power. The following list identifies the resources needed to allow teachers and students to make choices and decisions in a responsible way. If any of them are lacking, the administrator should find ways to make them available to everyone:

- *Information* that is required to do a job.
- *Skills* that are instrumental in accomplishing tasks.
- *An organization structure* that identifies and facilitates problem solving.
- *Understanding* effective problem solving methods.
- *Ability to communicate* one's point of view.
- *Organizational procedures* that aid in communication.
- *Tools* that are necessary to do one's job.
- *Material resources* sufficient to accomplish goals.

- *Ability to influence decisions* that affect one's own behavior.
- *Physical surroundings* that support required activities.
- *Physical and mental health.*
- *Money* over which people can exercise control.
- *Time* in which people can choose among alternative activities.

As a manager of human resources, you must maximize the extent to which you and your people have the above resources. Many organizational and personal problems arise when you don't.

6.332 Making opportunities available

A sense of power is frustrated and self-esteem is diminished if people can't use the resources at their command. If the significant decisions about your job were made by someone else, in spite of your years of training and experience, you would ultimately feel powerless and resentful. Teachers who can't use what they know because of policy constraints and ineffective organization will react similarly. Children find a way to undermine adult decisions, if they themselves are never allowed to make any decisions.

Human beings will sooner or later find a way to sabotage a system that doesn't allow them to exercise choices and decisions. Foot dragging, irresponsibility, lack of enthusiasm and poor morale can undermine a school as effectively as fire and bombs, and are more difficult to control.

In order to provide opportunities for people to exercise power, the following things are required in a school:

- Places and times where people interact, so that they can influence each other.
- Procedures that allow people to influence significant decisions.
- Occasions at which new skills can be learned.
- Role clarity, so that people know what responsibilities are theirs.
- A chance to share one's specialized knowledge with others.
- Clear goals, so that people know where to place their energies.

6.333 Capacities necessary to influence circumstances

The following is a list of the personal skills that are required in order for a person (adult or child) to feel an adequate sense of power. The absence or restriction of any one or more of them will reduce a person's self-esteem in situations that require those skills.

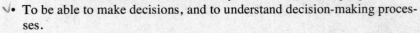

- To be able to communicate effectively so as to influence people.
- To be able to make decisions, and to understand decision-making processes.
- To have enough physical dexterity to manipulate the tools of one's trade.

- To know how to take responsibility.
- To be able to solve problems, and to understand problem-solving procedures.
- To be able to set goals and plan.
- To be able to use and demonstrate special skills.
- To be able to control one's emotions.
- To be able to set limits for oneself and others.

6.34   Models—How Beliefs and Standards Influence Self-Esteem

To have high self-esteem, a person must be able to refer to adequate human, philosophical, and operational models in order to establish meaningful goals, ideals, and personal standards.

- *Human models* are those persons we find to be worthy of emulation, or who have exemplary personal characteristics.
- *Philosophical models* are those sets of beliefs, assumptions, and inferences that we use to guide our behavior and judgments.
- *Operational models* are those mental patterns that guide how we perform our tasks.

These three types of models operate in any social system. In addition, people bring their personal models into all aspects of their behavior. In your school, teachers as well as students act in such ways as to exemplify the models they have. When personal models differ greatly, conflict can arise. Some models are more functional in some situations than others.

When the models a person has are not appropriate to a situation, the likelihood of punishment and failure increases, with a consequent reduction in self-esteem. People who have a wide array of models for reference points tend to be more flexible and adequate.

An organization such as a school can affect the self-esteem of its members (teachers and students) by increasing the availability of appropriate models for individual and group behavior.

6.341   Making human models available

People learn by seeing what other people do, and how they do it. Improving the conditions in which people can learn from each other requires that opportunities for observation of exemplary models be available.

In order to do this, the following things should be considered:

- You, as an administrator, are looked to as a model by your staff. If you wish then to be honest and open with each other, then they must *observe* you being so with them. If you wish them to take responsibility, then they must *observe* you assuming responsibilities. Too often, administrators are "hidden" from teachers, and cannot serve as models because of the lack of interaction with staff.

• Teachers can learn from each other if they have the opportunity to observe what each other does. Inter-class visitations should be arranged so that teachers who exemplify excellence in some aspect of their work can be observed by others.

• Inter-school visitations should be available so that your teachers can observe exemplary programs in other schools.

• Speakers and demonstrations should be brought to the school in order to suggest teaching alternatives to your staff.

• Central office administrators should talk to your staff periodically in order to lend a personal aspect to abstract policies, rules and regulations.

• Teachers, committees, and teams should have significant responsibilities in presenting issues and information in staff meetings.

6.342   Making philosophical models available

Schools are places in which many philosophical positions are made active. The way we deal with children's behavior reflects moral and ethical values held by teachers and administrators. What is taught reflects what is believed to be true and good for children to know. What we prepare children for is conditioned by our faith, hope, and vision of their future. We can clarify the assumptions on which programs and activities are based through the following ways:

• As an administrator, it is important that you clarify and share the beliefs that underlie your decisions and proposals.

• The staff of your school should, from time to time, meet together to share views about educational goals, as well as solving problems.

• Teachers should be encouraged to help children explore their values and beliefs through classroom activities.

• There should be a consistent and workable set of discipline procedures in your school.

• Tolerance for philosophical and personal differences should be a standard in your school.

6.343   Making operational models available

If a person must perform some task, but does not know how to do it well (absence of an operational model), the poorly done task will result in lowered self-esteem.

In addition to the usual teaching chores every teacher is required to do, there are fundamental models that are needed in order to perform adequately, many of which have already been described in previous sections.

• In your position as administrator, it is necessary that you identify areas of weakness in staff performance, and take steps to strengthen them.

• Staff members need to teach each other those skills that may be distributed unequally among them.

• A climate must be emphasized in which not knowing how to do something is seen as the absence of an operational model, rather than a personal fault.

• New learning opportunities should be made available to staff, and you, the administrator, must be an advocate for staff development.

6.4 HOW THE FOUR INGREDIENTS ARE APPLIED TO ALL SCHOOL ACTIVITIES

The following charts bring together the ideas explained above, and can be used as a checklist for evaluating the conditions for self-esteem as they exist in your school.

6.41 Their Use in Assessing Individuals and Their Behavior *? for mid-term*

If a problem with *connectiveness* exists, the following factors may be observed in a person's behavior:

_____ Is extremely shy
_____ Avoids new situations
_____ Belittles himself
_____ Disparages the importance of the group
_____ Excessively seeks group attention
_____ Feels lonely or alienated

If a problem with *uniqueness* exists, the following factors may be observed in a person's behavior:

_____ Exhibits extreme conformity or non-conformity
_____ Disparages his own worth or accomplishments
_____ Is uncomfortable with differences among people
_____ Reacts poorly to criticism
_____ Demands own way excessively
_____ Lacks imagination
_____ Rarely acts spontaneously or creatively

If a problem with *power* exists, the following factors may be observed in a person's behavior:

_____ Expresses helplessness and inadequacy
_____ Has an excessive need for control
_____ Has difficulty dealing with authority
_____ Is afraid to try new things
_____ Denies personal responsibility for own behavior
_____ Avoids leadership or makes excessive demands for it
_____ Demeans others and their accomplishments

If a problem with *models* exists, the following factors may be observed in a person's behavior:

_____ Is unclear about goals
_____ Communicates a poor self-image
_____ Is confused about his/her role
_____ Has excessive adoration of some person
_____ Acts inappropriately in social situations
_____ Is easily influenced or swayed
_____ Expresses feelings of hopelessness
_____ Vacillates about beliefs or commitments
_____ Makes excessive number of mistakes in whatever he does

6.42 How They Apply to Interpersonal Relationships

People who lack one or more of the ingredients of self-esteem will tend to act in characteristic ways in relationship to others. The problem may either arise from a personal deprivation—or *may result from the fact that the climate of the school undermines effective interpersonal relations*, and the factors in Section 6.43 need attention.

Where a problem with *connectiveness* exists, people will be likely to:

_____ Deny their commitment and responsibility to others
_____ Withhold approval of others
_____ Avoid intimacy or sharing of themselves
_____ Refuse to support group activities

Where a problem with *uniqueness* exists, people will be likely to:

_____ Be critical of others' personal characteristics
_____ Reject the fact that others are different or unique
_____ Demand that others adhere to abstract standards of behavior or performance
_____ Demean the creative accomplishments of others
_____ Categorize or label others too easily

Where a problem with *power* exists, people will be likely to:

_____ Be unwilling to share responsibility with others
_____ Be overly critical of others' accomplishments
_____ Demand that others submit to their authority
_____ Withhold resources that others need
_____ Undermine decisions that the group makes
_____ Refuse to be influenced by others, or to negotiate differences
_____ Unilaterally alter rules
_____ Take credit for others' accomplishments
_____ Give others responsibility while maintaining authority

Where a problem with *models* exists, people will be likely to:

_____ Keep personal agendas hidden
_____ Be unwilling to share opinions with others
_____ Refuse to clarify goals
_____ Behave in an inconsistent and unpredictable manner
_____ Disparage others' ideas and hopes
_____ Undermine others' enthusiasm
_____ Communicate feelings of hopelessness to others
_____ Be excessively pessimistic about group's plans

6.5 PROGRAMS AND ACTIVITIES TO RAISE SELF-ESTEEM

The following sections list many ways in which the four ingredients of self-esteem can be promoted in your school. All the ideas contained in this section have been tried successfully in some school or classroom. These are brief, but with imagination you and your teacher can fill in the details.

6.51 Enhancing Connectiveness

The following sections contain ideas for enhancing connectiveness among students and staff.

6.511 Enhancing connectiveness among students

a. *"Adopt a. . . ."* Each class "adopts" a younger class within the school to aid, go on outings with, tutor, give parties for, etc.

b. *"Radio."* If your school has a public address system, design radio programs to air school or community issues, as well as to reflect children's interests and styles.

c. *"Buttons."* Have special buttons, bearing the name and symbol of your school, made for children to wear. Have different colors for different classes.

d. *"Tutoring."* Emphasize cross-age tutoring, and use it extensively.

e. *"Coat of Arms."* Each class in your school designs a coat of arms, which is used on activity days or special occasions. Have one for the school.

f. *"Carnivals."* Have school carnivals or festivals several times a year. Keep them simple. Design activities for cross-age groups, and large group activities, i.e., "Which group of 50 children can make the loudest shout?"

g. *"Ancestor Days."* Special days in which children, individually or in groups, depict the style of life of their ancestors. Emphasize similarities, as well as differences, among the cultural backgrounds.

h. *"Awards."* Develop a large system of special awards, which are given from time to time. In addition to usual academic and athletic awards, try awards for cooperation, consideration, dress, being funny, etc. Give more than one award in each category.

i. *"Soup Day."* Get a big cauldron, have kids bring a vegetable, provide some soup bones. Boil up a big pot of vegetable soup. Have the kids all share in the school soup line; give your soup a name.

j. *"All-School Anythings."* Think up all sorts of things that everyone in the school can do on the same day: come in costumes, wear something red, paint a tatoo on face, everyone do something nice for someone, half the school blindfolded with the other half being helpers, or whatever. Have a committee of children decide the "Anything" of the month.

6.512   Enhancing connectiveness among staff

a. *"Share Meetings."* Devote one staff meeting a month to a few teachers' sharing some special feature that they are doing in their classes.

b. *"Secret Pals."* Have those who wish to participate draw a name from a hat; keep selections secret. Send special notes of commendation to each other; have each note mention something special about the Secret Pal. Announce Secret Pals at the end of the year.

c. *"Snacks."* Have staff take turns providing snacks for the staff room. Set the rule that they have to be made, not bought.

d. *"Visitations."* Provide the opportunity for staff to visit each other's classrooms on a regular basis.

e. *"Agenda Groups."* Have changing groups of staff members work with you to prepare the agenda for staff meetings.

f. *"Parties."* Arrange a weekend at a nearby resort. Have people bring their spouse or a friend. Have a good time, and plan to do it again in three months.

6.52   Enhancing Uniqueness

The following sections contain ideas for enhancing uniqueness within students and staff.

6.521   Enhancing uniqueness within students

a. *"Scavenger Room."* Get donations or scavenge all kinds of "junk." Have a room where kids can go to find things for their own individual creative projects.

b. *"Dress-Up Days."* Have students design individual costumes, work on them at school, and give lots of awards for special features and unique creations.

c. *"Show Boards."* Build outdoor kiosk to display special creations (art, poetry, stories) of children. Let everyone in the school be able to see them!

d. *"Me Day."* One day when everyone in the school focuses on himself— through writing stories or poems, art, sharing personal experiences with the class, values discussions, etc.

e. *"Frustration Pillows."* Purchase large pillow for each classroom. When children (or teachers) get angry or frustrated, they can hit the pillow.

f. *"Diaries."* Encourage use of diaries for all children in all classes. Have teachers allow time each day for children to write in them.

g. *"Feeling of the Day."* Decide on a feeling or quality that everyone in school will focus on for a day—through stories, discussions, writing. Feelings or qualities can be such things as courage, compassion, joy, anger, frustration, etc.

h. *"Guest Lecturers."* Have students with special skills, hobbies, or experiences be guest lecturers on the subject in another class.

6.522   Enhancing uniqueness within staff members

a. *"Pleasing Classrooms."* Encourage teachers to decorate their rooms in ways that are personally pleasing. They have to live in the room for a good part of the day!

b. *"Conferences."* Meet periodically with each of your teachers. Encourage them to tell you what special things they are doing in their classes. Don't evaluate; encourage them to define any problems they might be having.

c. *"Teaching Library."* Start a card catalogue of teaching ideas and materials available. Have every teacher contribute some special things which he or she does. Provide brief descriptions or categories, but in order to get the total idea, people have to go to the contributing teacher.

d. *"Bulletin Board."* Have each teacher be responsible for a display on the staff room bulletin board, on some topic of interest to the staff. Teachers can design it any way they wish.

e. *"Newsletters."* If you publish a staff newsletter (daily or weekly), be sure to acknowledge any special events occurring in teachers' classrooms.

f. *"Living Library."* Have each teacher list personal skills, hobbies, talents, interests, or special experiences. Print the compendium so that each person can be used as a resource for special projects in other classrooms.

6.53 Enhancing Power

The following sections contain ideas for enhancing student and staff "power."

6.531 Enhancing power by students

a. *"Activities Program."* Provide extracurricular activities programs one afternoon each week, using teachers, parents, volunteers. Give students a choice of activities. Survey the students to find out what they're interested in doing.

b. *"Token Economies."* Award tokens for predetermined, mutually agreed-upon activities. Tokens can be redeemed for privileges, goods, time off, etc. Have all-school projects, i.e., the school can buy a "free" afternoon of sports for 10,000 tokens!

c. *"Student Government."* Have a school government that includes teachers and students. Predetermine areas of responsibility. Encourage them to suggest rules and sanctions for the school. Provide some financial resources for them to make decisions about.

d. *"Decision Making."* Have a workshop for teachers about how to teach students to make decisions. Emphasize this skill in all the classes, gradually giving students more decision-making powers.

e. *"Complaint Court."* Set aside part of a week to hold court in your office. Students are free to come in to register complaints about any aspect of school life. Allow them to reserve the right of confidentiality.

f. *"Helpers."* Create a wide array of special duties in classrooms and in the school. Note carriers, eraser bangers, class monitors, principal's assistant, etc. Have students hold the positions for a limited time.

6.532 Enhancing power by teachers

a. *"Cabinet."* Have teachers elect representatives (grade level, function groups, etc.) to a Principal's Cabinet. The cabinet will prepare agendas for staff meetings, present complaints or grievances, review current problems, help set up ad hoc committees, plan school calendar, etc.

b. *"Evaluations."* Have each teacher evaluate self, prior to the principal's evaluation, using previously determined criteria or areas. Discuss discrepancies between their and your evaluation and seek to find a way to resolve the discrepancies.

c. *"Money."* Find a way to allow teachers to have control over money decisions through a form of unit budgeting, school budget committee, or special activities fund.

d. *"Committees."* See other sections of this Handbook for effective procedures for setting up working committees.

e. *"Teachers Teach Teachers."* Set aside one special staff meeting per month at which a teacher or small group of teachers are responsible for the agenda or program. Encourage those with special expertise to present inservice program for staff. Take a turn yourself.

f. *"Surveys."* Do a formal paper/pencil survey of staff attitudes from time to time. Ask what problems or stresses they see in the school. Let it be anonymous. Feed back results of the survey to the staff.

6.54 Enhancing Models

The following sections contain ideas for enhancing a sense of models for students and staff.

6.541 Enhancing models for students

a. *"Community Resource File."* Survey parents, local agencies, and the local community. Develop a file of "special resources"—people who are experts, specialists, have esoteric talents, or whom children should know. Bring these "special people" to the school as classroom or project resources.

b. *"Values Clarification."* Have a workshop for teachers on values clarification techniques. Emphasize the importance of looking at values that exist in the school.

c. *"Behavior Manual."* Develop a school discipline system. Prepare a manual for students and parents about school rules, standards, and sanctions. Have classroom sessions so that students understand the manual.

d. *"Culture Week."* Have a week in which the whole school studies, plays, and acts as if it were in another time or place. Encourage students to learn about another society or culture, and experience it themselves.

e. *"Special Behavior Days."* From time to time have a day when a certain kind of behavior is emphasized—tolerance, compassion, honesty, helpfulness, etc. Have classroom discussions, lessons, readings on the subject. Have children discuss how it felt by the end of the day.

f. *"Student Teachers."* Many children tend to learn more effectively from each other. Use learning teams, tutors, student presentations in classes, sharing sessions in all classes in your school.

6.542   Enhancing models for staff members

a. *"Focus Activities."* Take leadership to promote a central focus for the school year, in which all staff participate. Such things as raising self-esteem, dealing with hard-to-reach children, improving reading scores, can serve as a unifying theme for the staff. Inservice courses, school resources, resource teachers, etc., are all focused on the theme.

b. *"Staff Meetings."* Make staff meetings a model for effective group action. Participate fully in all staff discussions and activities.

c. *"Wise Persons."* Write to a lot of well-known people, both within the field of education and in other fields, i.e., politics, writing, etc., with whom your staff would be interested in speaking. Invite them to your school, when they might be in the area, and have them discuss things with your staff. Write to enough people so that some will be free to pay a visit.

d. *"School Calendar."* Have a very large calendar in the staff room on which all upcoming events are easily seen. Include special events in individual classrooms. Let everyone know what's happening.

See also Sections 6.512 (a) and (d), 6.522 (c) and (f), and 6.532 (e).

7

How to Improve
Relations with
Parents and Community

This chapter describes how to maximize the role of parents as a valued resource for your school, and provides methods for dealing with some of the problems you may have with parents. Increasing parental involvement will have far-reaching benefits for your school.

7.1 INVOLVING PARENTS IN SCHOOL PROGRAMS AS VOLUNTEER AIDES

This section will help you consider using unpaid, parent volunteer aides.

7.11 How to Recruit Parent Volunteers

It may take one to two years of groundwork to develop a "tradition" of parents volunteering. When this tradition is established, parents themselves will be your best recruiters. Sections 7.2, 7.3 and other parts of this Handbook describe ways to increase parents' sense of being an active part of the school.

Both you and your staff can consciously build a positive climate where parents feel they are needed in the school. Parents will want to participate if they feel they are really helping the programs and their children. In some com-

151

munities, negative attitudes toward the school may be an impediment to volunteering, making the need for the program all the more apparent.

The following recruitment strategies will work best if used in combinations that are appropriate for your school and community situation.

1. You and your staff should assess the need for parent aides in your school: How many? Doing what jobs? For how long during the school day? In what classes or parts of the school?

Develop a list of these needs, being as specific as possible. Clarify general skills parent volunteers must have, such as "Should like children," "Likes to be helpful," "Enjoys teaching children." Requiring many specialized skills will scare off parents. Add to this list some of the rewards for volunteering; for example: "Taking a part in improving the school's program," "Helping children move further in their learning," "Experiencing the joys of teaching."

Combine the above lists in an interesting, readable communication and send it to the parents.

2. Select a few dedicated parents and establish a Parent Volunteer Committee. Work with them to establish procedures for recruitment. They can handle most of the responsibilities (communication, coordination) for this.

3. Telephone parents and ask them to volunteer. Direct recruitment emphasizes the importance of the school's need, and encourages volunteering.

4. Have an event that brings the parents to the school, such as a potluck dinner, back to school night, or children's program. Deliver a talk about the need for parent volunteers, with time for questions and answers.

5. The need for volunteers should be regularly mentioned in your school's newsletter or other communications to parents. Include biographical sketches of your volunteers, with their comments on volunteering.

6. Ask parents who are presently volunteers to recruit their friends and neighbors, including those without children in the school.

7. Ask teachers about parents who show special interest in the school. Have the teacher ask them to volunteer, or contact the parent yourself.

8. Emphasize effective and positive parent relations with your staff. Devote inservice time to this subject.

7.12 How to Make a Talent Survey of Parents

Parents can be school resources by taking advantage of their special skills, talents, interests, and hobbies. A dentist might help a unit on dental hygiene. A carpenter might have scrap lumber for art projects. An artist could develop interesting art lessons.

Every school has parents with useful skills. You need to know who they are and what they do. A talent survey provides this information. (See Figure 7-1.)

[EXAMPLE OF TALENT SURVEY]

Dear Parents,

Do you do something or know about something that children in our school can profit from? Children eagerly learn when exposed to people who are experts in doing things that they are learning. Among our parents are many experts. We need to use your experience to improve the quality of education for all of our children.

Please consider becoming part of our Parent Expert Program (P.E.P.), so your talents, skills, and hobbies will benefit our programs. We are making a file of parents who are willing to be called on by our teachers when expert help is needed. If you are willing to be a P.E.P. expert, please complete the attached form, and you will be called when your special interest is needed. Even if you don't have much time available, you may have useful information when a teacher needs it. We all look forward to your becoming part of Washington School's P.E.P. program.

Sincerely yours,
Joselyn McGrath, Principal

. . . .

Tear this portion off and mail or deliver to the school office.
NAME _____TELEPHONE#_____
ADDRESS _____
1. What type of work do you do? _____
2. Where do you work? _____
3. What special interests or hobbies do you have that you would be willing to share with interested children? _____
_____
4. Have you traveled in or outside the United States? If so, where?
_____
5. Have you ever been a teacher? If so, what grade(s)? _____
What subjects? _____
6. Please check any special interests, experiences or hobbies that are not covered above. Don't be shy; the range of interests of our teachers and students is very broad.

____ Art (specify ____   ____ Carpentry   ____ Craft work (specify
_____)   ____ Gardening   _____)
____ Medical fields   ____ Science (specify   ____ Government
____ Home arts   _____)   ____ Story telling
____ Sports, dance, etc.   ____ Other: _____   ____ Other: _____
(specify _____)   ____ Other: _____   ____ Other: _____

FIGURE 7-1

7.13 How to Increase Parent Satisfaction as Volunteers

Recruiting volunteers is one problem; keeping them is another. Volunteering should be so satisfying to parents that they encourage others to do so, spreading positive feelings about the school.

The following things can be done to make a volunteer's job more rewarding:

• Make each volunteer's job specific and manageable. When a person knows precisely what to do, and how to do it, job satisfaction goes up. At one school a volunteer became known as the "Spelling Lady." She went to different classrooms, drilled the children on their weekly spelling list, and gave each room its weekly test. Children seeing her at other times would ask about words and show off the "harder" words they had learned. She became a valued resource to the children and their teachers.

• Encourage teachers to tell volunteers about things they observe them do. It's important that praise be given for specific things a volunteer has done well. Have teachers and volunteers meet for lunch or during recess. Encourage the teachers to view volunteers as part of a "teaching team."

• When a volunteer has been in a class for a while, have the children write thank-you notes for her help. Put them in a scrapbook, and present it to the volunteer.

• Parent volunteers enjoy and benefit from "professional treatment." Have several inservice sessions during the year to upgrade skills in relating to children and teaching.

• Volunteers like to know that the principal notices them. Meet with volunteers individually or in groups. Let them know that you believe they are doing important work.

• Have a "Volunteer of the Week." In a display area or the school newsletter, have a biographical sketch of a volunteer. Let other parents know about the role of volunteers in the school program.

• If you have a Parent Volunteer Committee, be sure that its members survey the attitudes of volunteers from time to time. Identify gripes and satisfactions. Let the volunteers know that someone cares—and will take action to correct what is not going smoothly.

• Have a volunteer babysitting service at the school, supervised by parents with assistance from older students.

• Be sure volunteers are welcomed in the teachers' room. Have them bring their own coffee cup. Help them feel part of the staff.

7.14 How to Use Parent Volunteers Most Effectively

1. Assess teachers' needs before placing volunteers in classrooms. Have job descriptions for volunteers.

2. If volunteer tasks are diverse, have the teacher develop "job cards" for different functions. This will diminish confusion or poor communications.

3. Give volunteers some training in effective teacher/child relations. If there is no specific task to do, they can still be with children in a positive way.

4. You, a teacher, and her volunteers should meet initially to clarify the teacher's expectations and to answer questions the new volunteers may have.

5. Familiarize volunteers with the school's program as a whole. Let them know what is happening in other classrooms. Knowing about school programs and goals will make their job more meaningful.

6. Have parents who are willing to be "substitute volunteers." If a parent can't show up, try to have a replacement. Teachers get frustrated if volunteers don't meet schedules.

7. Emphasize the need for punctuality and regularity. Make these criteria for continued participation in the volunteer program.

8. Have a document titled "Standards for Volunteers" in which there are guidelines for effective volunteering and criteria for participation. If parents do not meet criteria, discontinue their services, if discussion or training does not help.

7.2 HOW THE SCHOOL CAN HAVE ITS OWN PUBLIC RELATIONS PROGRAM

A community that is unhappy with its schools drains the enthusiasm and creativity of administrators and teachers, and undermines the commitment of children to learn. Parents cannot support what they don't understand. A school community that feels that its interests are being met will be supportive and active. In this section are ways to build community support for your program.

7.21 Giving Something to the Parents: Parent Education

Parent education programs that are well run and relate to the interests of parents will build good will in the community. Assessing parent needs and organizing resources to meet them is the first step to a good parent education program.

7.211 How to determine parent needs

Familiarize yourself with the resources that are available to parents in your community. These may include:

Family Service Agency	Adult Education	Church-Family Program
Community Mental Health Program	Juvenile Probation Department	Educational Diagnostic Services
Psychiatric and Psychological Services	University Extension Programs	Community College Social Welfare Service

What do people who are engaged in these programs have to say about parent and family needs in the community? Do parents utilize these services? If there are few such programs available, the field may be open for you to generate a variety of parent education programs.

Survey by questionnaire the parents in your school, and have them tell you what programs they would like. How you ask questions on a survey will determine the quality of the response.

Questions about interest:

Would you like to attend a parent education program?
Do you feel that a program for parents is needed?
Have you attended such programs in the past?
Are you interested in a school-sponsored parent education program?
Do you think the school should sponsor such a program?

Questions about content:

Offer alternatives; do not leave it to the parents to describe what they want. Leave room for their suggestions. Program examples:

Raising Self-Esteem	Parent Discussion Group
Setting Rules and Limits	Communicating With Children
Discipline	Special Problems
Emotional Problems of Children	Child Development
Helping Children do Better in School	Common Childhood Ailments and How to Treat Them
Handling Lying and Stealing	Teaching Children About Sex
Helping a Child to Be Creative	Doing Play Therapy with Children
Parent Effectiveness Training	Program on School Curriculum

Questions about format:

____Lectures	____Small-group discussions
____Afternoons	____Evenings
____Once a week	____Once a month
____Will babysitting be needed?	

If you have a PTA or Home-School Club, use the committee of that group as a sounding board for ideas. Encourage them to assess the interests of parents. Make them responsible for promoting parent education programs.

7.212 How to set up parent education programs

• If your school has not had parent education programs, it may take time to develop the idea that the school is a resource for adults. Initially, reaction may be minimal. Parents will take advantage of the resource if it remains available and well publicized.

• Plan a program for the year. One or two programs a year may be sufficient for your school. Have them well organized so parents know what to expect. Set dates early, and consider conflicts such as holidays, other school or community events, etc.

• Work closely with the PTA, Parent Advisory Committee, Home-School Club, or other group. Give major responsibility for promotion to this group.

• When parent interests have been assessed, and decisions about programs made, investigate the personnel available in your community. See Section 7.211 for a list of agencies to contact. Get speakers with prior experience in similar programs.

• Talk with your local adult education department, community college or university extension officials. Funds may be available to pay instructors for your parent education program. Parents may find a "course" more acceptable than "just a lecture at the school."

• Be a publicist. Have catchy titles for the program and use colorful advertising handbills. Give notice long before the events, with follow-up announcements as reminders. Have parents make a prior commitment to attend.

• Provide evaluation forms after each session. Allow parents to feel that their opinions influence the design of the program. Use their feedback for future planning.

• Parents want practical advice or ideas. Avoid abstract or highly intellectual programs. Select your speakers or instructors with this in mind.

7.213 How to publicize parent education programs

See Section 7.22 on Written Communications.

• All media should be considered. In a town which has a daily or weekly newspaper, an article about the program will add importance to it. Local radio stations provide public service announcements, without cost. In large cities, such media may be less useful, unless the program is for the general public.

• Handbills, designed to be eye catching, can be sent home with children and placed in local stores. Written communications are more often brought home by younger children than by older ones. The mail is more likely to insure delivery, although cost may be prohibitive.

• Word of mouth is an effective way to inform people. A phone-calling crew may be a real help, followed by a printed description.

• Have children make posters to publicize the event. Placing the posters in public places makes children feel important, as well as getting your message across.

• Many schools have difficulty getting fathers to attend school programs. Consider special topics or approaches that would appeal to fathers. At one school in northern California, fathers rarely came to school events. The principal noted that fathers liked to meet for a beer after work. A hall near the school was used for a "beer party" to which many fathers came. The school's program was explained, and the fathers participated in a question-and-answer session about the school.

• Be imaginative and consider *your* community. One school placed a public address system on a flat bed truck. Teachers and children toured the community, handing out free lemonade and handbills about their parent education program.

7.22 Informing the Parents: Written Communications

Written communications will remain the most frequent method for giving information to parents. This section suggests ways to make written communication more effective.

7.221 How to enhance the quality of written communications

Consider the kinds of written communications that you could send to parents:

A. *Personal Notes:* An important way to personalize and communicate special interest in a child. Avoid being critical. Send home notes with a positive tone. See Figure 7-2.

Dear Mr. and Mrs. Smith:
    I just wanted to let you know that Kenny has been making greater efforts during recent weeks. While he has not turned everything in on time, he has finished several assignments. His recent math quiz, on which he scored 70%, was the highest grade of the year for him. Your continued encouragement of him seems to be paying off! It's O.K. to let him know about this note.

                                       Regards,
                                       Ethel McRay, Principal

---

FIGURE 7-2

B. *Announcements of School Events:* Visual attraction is very important. Use colored paper, illustrations, large print for emphasis.

C. *Commendation Notes:* Have them printed ahead of time. Give them out freely to take home. Encourage your teachers to use them, also—parents love to hear good things about their children. See Figure 7-3.

---

* * * * * SPECIAL COMMENDATION * * * * *

Be it known that _____ has done something special that parents, teachers, and the student him/herself should be proud of.

On this day _____ of _____, 19___, this student

_____

_____

Signed: _____

Teacher

FIGURE 7-3

D. *Formal Letters:* Be sure they are printed well. Important messages are demeaned when they are poorly printed. Keep them limited to one page.

E. *School Calendars:* Parents like to know what's happening at school. Even though many may not be able to attend events, it increases their sense of connection to the school to know about them. Children often do not tell parents about events at school.

F. *Program Descriptions:* Let the parents know about what the school is doing. When a new reading program is adopted, tell parents what it's called (it's handy to have a name); give a *brief* description of its special features; say what it's supposed to do and why it was adopted.

G. *Permission Slips:* Parents usually need to give special permission for school outings, programs, etc. Keep explanations simple, but complete. Use clear, large printing. Have a detachable form to sign. Encourage parents to call for more information.

H. *School Newsletter:* See Section 7.222.

Other things to consider:

• Find out if there is a parent in your school who has had experience in publicity or public relations. He or she may be willing to volunteer to prepare written communications in a pleasing way. You might have your own (free) public relations department!

• Avoid educational jargon in communications. Don't assume that parents are familiar with abbreviations such as E.C.E., S.R.A., L.D.G.

• Be aware of your own writing style, and alter it to fit different circumstances. Work on being concise.

7.222 Periodic newsletter: what to include

1. A regular newsletter to parents can pay dividends. Securing parent volunteers, getting special resources, promoting a positive climate when bond or tax-override elections occur, and having parents who support the school and its staff can be the results of a good newsletter.

2. Parent volunteers can "take charge" of the newsletter, under your supervision. Some parents want to help the school, but not in the classroom.

3. Have a regular format, masthead, and style, so that it is easily identified as being from your school.

4. An appealing format will help to distinguish the newsletter from junk mail. A good-looking publication will be left on coffee tables or magazine racks so that others will read it.

5. These are the things that can be included in a newsletter:

—announcements of meetings and events
—biographical sketches of you, teachers, volunteers, or other school personnel
—letters from parents
—special classroom activities
—reports of field trips or special events
—children's writings and drawings
—pictures and illustrations
—debates about educational practices
—editorials about educational issues
—current books for children
—announcements of nearby classes for parents
—types of volunteers needed by the school
—"thank-you's" for special things parents have done for the school
—short articles or reprints about parenting practices

7.23 Making Parents Happy: Special Programs

Parents want to know that the school is helping their children. When parents see children being productive and happy, their regard for the school and its staff increases. When parents have good experiences at the school, their support increases.

7.231 Showing off the children

• Use children's work (writing and art) in the school's newsletter, and to illustrate or dramatize other communications. Give credits to the students.

• Have students prepare announcements of school events, which go to parents or are for public display.

• Include a children's performance at programs for parents, such as PTA meetings, parent education programs, etc. The children may reperform something they did in class (a play, singing, a reading). This will encourage parent attendance.

• Literary magazines, art books, school and class newspapers should be produced and sent home. These are examples of productivity which parents value.

• Report notable events in the childrens' school life in the newsletter or in special announcements.

• Announce class or school officers in parent communications.

7.232 Food and fun—a winning combination

• Always include coffee, cookies, etc., at parent events. Have coffee and tea available to parents who visit the school. Parents are not offended if a small donation for refreshments is asked for at special events.

• Have different classrooms prepare an International Food Bazaar. Invite parents to it. It's helpful to school/parent relations, and a good social studies unit for the children.

• Many schools surveyed by the authors said that food-related events bring more parents to school than informational events. Potluck dinners, barbeques, spaghetti feeds, Mexican food festivals, etc., provide occasions at which lots of parents can become familiar with the school. One small school in a rural area, in which most parents were poor and undereducated, never had parents come to informational meetings, but always had at least 90 percent attendance at potluck dinners.

7.233 How to get parents to show up

The previous sections of this chapter contain many ideas for increasing parent participation. A review of the principles includes:

1. Parents are the most important extra-school resource available to you. ✻

2. The goal is to make active participation in the school a "tradition." This takes time but, when established, allows the community itself to reinforce its interest in your school.

3. All communications to parents should stimulate interest and gain attention.

4. Parent participation is strengthened if your teaching staff actively participates in the process.

5. Interest in children's education increases if parents get something of value from the school.

7.3 HOW TO FIND OUT WHAT THE COMMUNITY WANTS FROM THE SCHOOL

There are two ways to find out what parents want from the school. One is by asking parents to report in written form (questionnaires); the other is through face-to-face contact.

7.31 Designing and Using Questionnaires

Advantages:

- Possible anonymity
- Much information acquired for low expenditure of your time
- Responses are organized in a usable manner
- Everyone has the same opportunity to respond
- Reduces the effect of a vocal minority
- Permits planning and forethought to data collection

Disadvantages:

- Returns may be a small percentage of parents
- Limited opportunity to clarify issues

Suggestions on how to use questionnaires:

- Make questionnaire brief. Orient it to a single topic if possible.
- Make the questionnaire easy to read and aesthetically pleasing.
- Provide feedback to parents about the results of the questionnaire as soon as possible. People need to know that information has been used.
- Use language that the average parent can understand. Avoid jargon and educational terminology.
- Tell parents *how* information obtained from the questionnaire will be used.
- Provide a simple way for the questionnaire to be returned.
- Keep the questionnaire on one sheet of paper, even if it must be large and folded.
- Consider sampling; select every fifth name on the roster. Emphasize selectivity to parents.

7.311 How to design questions

Evaluative questions should enable a parent to judge observable behavior, preferably in his own child.

POOR: Do you approve of the school's current reading program? _____ *yes* _____ *no*

GOOD: Does it seem to you that your child has more interest and/or skill in reading? _____ *yes* _____ *no*

POOR: Do you think that discipline at school is adequate? _____ *yes* _____ *no*

GOOD: Have you seen or heard anything that would lead you to feel that discipline is a problem at our school? _____ *yes* _____ *no* If yes, what? _____

POOR: Do you think that the school is doing an overall good job? _____ *yes* _____ *no*

GOOD: Does your child seem comfortable and satisfied with school? _____ *yes* _____ *no* _____ *somewhat*

Questions about program should be designed so that parents can choose among alternatives:

POOR: What subjects should be emphasized in the program? _____
GOOD: Among the following subjects, check the three which you feel are most important:

___Reading	___Art	___Science
___Math	___Writing	___Social Studies
___P.E.	___Public Speaking	___ Spelling

POOR: What do you feel should be added to the present program? _____
GOOD: Among the list below are subjects that could be added to our program. Show which ones you would like to see added. Place a (1) before the one you would most like to see, (2) before the next, and (3) before the next.

___Art	___Drama	___Public Speaking
___Creative Writing	___Music	___Crafts
___Science	___Other:_____	___Other: _____

There should be one or two open-ended questions on each questionnaire, so that parents can add things that are not included in your survey:

"Please use this space for any other comments you would like to make."
"If we have not asked about something that concerns you, please tell us about it."
"What else would you like us to know?"

7.32   Using Direct Contact

Some advantages to using direct contact are:

- You can explore issues in depth.
- You can work toward solutions with the people who are involved.
- Attitudes and feelings can be expressed fully.
- It is possible to respond immediately to parents' concerns.

Some disadvantages to using direct contact are:

- Vocal subgroups may monopolize the process, unless there is agreement to discussion rules.
- Participation is limited to those who can attend.
- You can't determine the attitudes of those who aren't present.

7.321   Meetings

See Section 9.4 on conducting meetings.

7.322   One-to-one contact

The principal and staff of a suburban elementary school needed more parent aides to help a program of individualized instruction. Announcements and letters did not produce many volunteers. The principal spent a good part of her time during one week calling over 200 families, explaining the problem to them. By the end of the week she had 70 committed volunteers, and the program was launched.

Sometimes direct contact with parents is the only way to get a message across. It is time consuming, and administrators are diffident about talking with parents whom they don't know personally.

Some parents are especially interested and knowledgeable about school affairs. Many of them may be important members of your local community. Their opinions may represent a broad segment of local parents, and they can become important sounding boards for new ideas.

Parents become interested in the school if they believe that the *school is interested in them*. A positive encounter with some parents begins the process of having people feel that you are interested in what they have to say.

Meeting one to one with parents who are critical of the school's program gives an opportunity to build a personal relationship, and to explore differences in depth.

Don't feel that parents must always meet in your office. Meeting on the parent's "ground" can create a positive climate for relationships.

Often your most bitter critic may only be seeking to have a personal relationship with you so that he or she can feel that you are listening. It is useful to make special efforts with such people. Even if no resolution occurs, you can show that you have done your part.

7.323 Coffee klatches

Meeting informally with small groups of parents is a useful way to get information to the community, and feedback from it. There are key parents who can arrange "coffees" to which ten to 12 parents can be invited. This is especially useful if you are a new administrator in the community.

- Encourage parents to express their views candidly.
- Share something of yourself with the parents, so that they know something personal about you.
- Be prepared to tell them something about the school's program, especially something that you want to "sell."

7.4 ORGANIZING PARENT ADVISORY GROUPS

Across the country there is increased interest in involving parents in managing and monitoring school programs. Federal programs in compensatory education, state programs in early childhood and multi-cultural education, and local district efforts often mandate Parent Advisory Committees. Many districts have found that giving parents a large influence in the schools is the only way to insure adequate tax and bonding support. This section describes methods for creating Parent Advisory Groups, and suggests ways to help them become important resources for program development.

7.41 Defining Purposes

Parent participation often flounders on the issue of "what are we here for." Clarifying purposes will serve to focus energies.

7.411 Some possible purposes for a school's parent advisory group

1. To provide a channel for bringing parental concerns and interests before the school, and vice versa.
2. To advise the school about finding and using community resources.
3. To coordinate recruitment of parent and community resources for the school, i.e., parent volunteers, materials, etc.
4. (In areas where ethnic or racial minorities are predominant.) To help the

school to understand cross-cultural effects of school programs, and the needs of groups affected by the school.

5. To help define the school's goals and objectives.

6. To lobby school boards and other public bodies as advocates of the school.

7. To work with you and the staff to evaluate programs, especially those with specific relevance to the local community.

√ 7.412 Some possible problems you are likely to encounter

1. Confusion about what the group is to do, and how it is to do it.

2. Vague guidelines from local, state, or federal bodies that mandate the Parent Advisory Group.

3. Staff resistance to threats implied by parent evaluation of their classrooms.

4. Conflicting opinions among parents and staff about the purposes of the group.

5. Unwillingness of parents and/or staff to serve on the group.

√ 7.413 Some things to consider when dealing with purposes and problems

• You need to take the initiative to help the Parent Advisory Group determine its goals and objectives.

• Advise the group to set objectives for the year that are concrete and capable of being evaluated at year's end.

• Your staff needs to provide input about the group's goals.

• When goals and objectives are determined, they should be clear, written, and publicly announced to parents and staff (see Chapter 2 on goal setting).

• Distinguish between goals and objectives.

• Find out how other schools or districts have organized Parent Advisory Groups. Bring such information to the attention of yours.

• Invite parents or administrators from other schools or districts that have Parent Advisory Groups to speak to your parents.

• Work out *your* relationship to the Parent Advisory Group. Consider taking a "subordinate" but influential role, such as executive secretary.

7.42 How Members Can Be Selected or Recruited

Check guidelines from federal, state, or local programs that may mandate Parent Advisory Groups. Some programs specify the manner in which members of these groups are to be selected. If there are none:

1. Start with parents who have previously indicated interest in the school. Encourage them to join at the same time as you are soliciting volunteers from the entire parent body.

2. Depending on the size of the Parent Advisory Group, you may choose to start with a small group, to which are gradually added parents who represent more of the parents in your school.

3. Publicize the need for parents through a newsletter, which describes the purposes of the group. Coffee klatches and one-to-one meetings are also useful recruitment methods.

4. In areas where the parents tend to know each other, elections may be used. In other places, the process is best started by the administrator, staff, and a small group of parents.

5. Clarify in writing the requirements for parents who serve. Duties, obligations, time commitments, meetings, etc., should be spelled out so that parents know what they are expected to do.

6. If there is community conflict about the school, *avoid* "packing" the Parent Advisory Group with supporters. This will only serve to increase community dissension, and undermine the value of the group as spokesman for the parents. Having varied opinions represented on the Parent Advisory Group allows the disagreements to be explored.

7. You must act to dispel the idea that the Parent Advisory Group is an adversary to you and the school.

8. Plan meetings in order that fathers may participate. This means that evenings need to be set up. If the work of the Parent Advisory Group is only to be during the day, it mainly limits personnel to non-working mothers.

9. Consider babysitting needs of members, and provide this in the recruitment stage.

10. Find more parents who are willing to serve than are needed. Parents drop out, and it is useful to know ready replacements.

7.43 How to Facilitate Effective Parent Advisory Meetings

You will quickly find that there is a dilemma about your role vis-a-vis the Parent Advisory Group in your school. In order to overcome this you should:

• Define your role initially. Establish an agreement, between yourself and the group, about your relationship. This may change as time and experience require.

• Your role as facilitator will be important. You have information that the Parent Advisory Group needs. You can offer advice about how to perform their functions, how to conduct meetings, and how to use the resources of the school and district.

• Clarify the distinction between "advising" and "managing" so that members of the group do not interfere with your responsibilities in the school.

• Many Parent Advisory Groups experience problems in conducting meetings. Prepare a simple set of guidelines for meetings and recommend it to the group.

• Suggest outside consultants to work with the Parent Advisory Group in its formative states.

7.44 Relations between Parent Advisory Group and Staff

Maintaining good relations between a Parent Advisory Group and your staff will ultimately be looked at as your problem. You will have to be the link between the two.

7.441 Possible problem areas

• Lack of staff understanding about the purposes and goals of the Parent Advisory Group.

• Separation of Parent Advisory Group and staff with no staff participation in its work.

• Having a strong, antagonistic parent or group of parents on the Parent Advisory Group.

• The goals of the group being significantly different from those of the staff.

• Lack of information to both groups about the needs, procedures, and functions of the other.

• The administrator taking problems to one group which should be addressed to the other, e.g., discussing a personnel problem with the Parent Advisory Group when it should be done with the staff.

7.442 Ways to avoid these problems

• Have one or two staff members, selected by the staff, serve as liaison with the Parent Advisory Group.

• Invite Parent Advisory Group members to staff meetings in which they can participate. Design the agenda so that confidential matters are not dealt with, and have items to which group members can contribute.

• Determine what information needs to be passed between staff and Parent Advisory Group, and create a method for insuring that it does; e.g., distribute minutes of group meetings to staff.

• At staff meetings, from time to time, have concerns about the Parent Advisory Group discussed by the staff.

• Solicit staff permission to have Parent Advisory Group members visit classrooms, then invite parents to do so.

• See chapters on Conflict Resolution and Problem Solving.

• Encourage the Parent Advisory Group to have as one of its goals assisting the staff in accomplishing school goals. Survey staff for needs that the group can meet.

• Organize informal get-togethers between staff and Parent Advisory Group: parties, potlucks, or joint sponsorship of some activity for the children.

7.5   DEALING WITH MINORITY GROUPS

Relations between minority groups and schools are complex and often stressful. In this section, we will touch on some features of the problem. Other sections of this chapter and of the Handbook itself are applicable to dealing with parents who are members of minority groups. We will not reiterate things that are amplified in other sections.

7.51   Establishing Bridges Between School and Minority Parents

Things to do, and things to think about:

Have your staff make-up include members from the minorities that your school serves. Bilingualism and special language/cultural compensatory programs often result from decisions that are made above the local school level, i.e., central office, school board, county, state or federal offices of education. You should nevertheless be an active participant in policy decisions about these matters, based on your understanding and sensitivity to local needs and conditions.

You and your staff, by becoming involved in local community activities, will show that you care about the local community and its heritage. Ask parents with whom you have a good relationship to "sponsor" your access to such activities.

In areas where special ethnic or racial groups predominate, the school should actively demonstrate its respect for and interest in those groups. This can be done in specific ways:

a. Written communications should be translated into languages used locally, especially if English is a second language to many parents.

b. Newsletters, special announcements, etc., should be illustrated in ways that depict local ethnic motifs.

c. Parents who come to school should see pictures, signs, and decorations that symbolize the major local ethnic groups.

d. Special recognition should be given to ethnic heroes and holidays (Cinco de Mayo, Martin Luther King Day, etc.) by having special classroom or all-school activities.

e. Parents should be surveyed to assess their interest in special cultural programs or multi-cultural learning activities. Let them know that the school believes there is much in their heritage which children should know.

f. Make a special effort to establish a personal relationship with parents in your school who are local community leaders. They can be useful sounding boards for ideas, and can clarify conflicts that emerge.

g. Have adult translators available when large percentages of parents prefer another language. Avoid using children as translators.

h. Start to learn the local language (whether foreign, a dialect, or "street talk"). Check out your competence with sympathetic adults (staff or parents).

i. Learn local customs about visiting and neighborliness. When visiting parents, be tactful. Don't assume that ethnic or racial miniorities are either very much the same as or very much different from you. Respect differences *and* similarities.

j. Familiarize yourself with the culture and history of the minority groups you serve. Know the recent history of such groups in your community. Such information will help you with children and parents.

k. Avoid having the local minorities represented on your staff only at the lowest levels, i.e., paraprofessional aides, custodians, et al.

l. See Section 7.4 on Parent Advisory Groups.

7.52 Setting Up Multi-Cultural Programs

Because of the diversity of needs and programs relative to different groups, this section will only suggest some things to think about. There is a growing literature about multi-cultural education, and you should learn from exemplary projects in other districts.

• Make use of local resources, including parents, as much as possible. Wide variations exist within groups in attitudes about the place of ethnic education in schools. Staying close to local resources allows your school to more closely represent local interests.

• Encourage your teachers to help each other with information, materials, and resources. In a culturally diverse staff, some will be more familiar with multi-cultural materials than others.

• Specific activities, special programs, and teaching units are best accepted if they reflect the intention to promote a multi-cultural climate in the school (see Section 7.51 and Chapter 6 on Self-Esteem).

• Apart from mandated programs, allow variation in how your teachers use multi-cultural materials. Some will be more comfortable in this area of the curriculum than others.

• Invite teachers from other programs to inservice sessions with your staff. Your teachers will profit from the practical experiences of others.

• The transition to a multi-cultural school will be gradual. Evidencing continued concern and adding new features periodically will be required in order to convince the community of the school's sincerity.

7.53   Dealing with Staff Prejudices   √

Staff prejudices about minority group children and parents can be a source of friction within the school, and between it and the community. Expect some degree of prejudice within your staff, which may be composed largely of people who are not members of local minority groups.

Prejudice may be either conscious or unconscious, and arises from two sources:

1. Those prejudices which result from some bad experience(s) which a person has had with a member or members of some special group, and which have become emotionally generalized to all members of that group.

2. Those prejudices which arise from misinformation or lack of information about the special characteristics of members of ethnic or racial groups.

You have a special responsibility to deal with staff prejudices (and your own) if your school has minority group students. You can do the following things about both types of prejudice:

1. Encourage home visits by yourself and your teachers. Do not leave such visits only to special community liaison workers. If you have such aides in your school, have teachers make home visits with them as much as possible.

2. Have regular inservice sessions about ways to work effectively with the specific minorities in your community.

3. If your school has programs that mandate minority group aides, provide time for three kinds of meetings:

   a. Meetings of teacher and an aide with you to discuss classroom procedures, activities, and roles.

   b. Meetings of the aides in which they can share experiences, air grievances, and communicate perceptions.

   c. Combined meetings of the teachers and aides, especially at inservice sessions about cultural issues.

4. Provide a staff library of books on multi-cultural education, especially works about your local minority groups.

5. Openly discuss the likelihood of unconscious prejudice among the staff. Redefine such prejudice as a lack of information, rather than a moral problem.

6. When you fear that a staff member is acting in ways that imply prejudice, have a conference with that teacher to discuss such behavior. The risk you take in doing this may diminish the greater risk of community reaction.

7. If you have teachers who are truly uncomfortable with parents and/or children of a minority group, raise the possibility of transfer, and help the teacher to do so.

8. Familiarize yourself with the ethos of local minority groups so that you can facilitate your teachers' awareness of cultural differences and similarities.

7.6 DEALING WITH PARENTS OF PROBLEM CHILDREN

Working with parents whose children are problems at school is a stressful part of your job. This section will help you alleviate some problems and handle others more effectively.

7.61 Clarifying the School's Expectations and Standards

• Your school should have a manual that describes the rules, behavioral expectations, and standards for both parents and children. Such a base line will help parents understand staff expectations.

• Invite new families to discuss the manual with you so as to clarify the school's policies.

• Consequences for rule infractions should be defined in the manual so that parents and children are not surprised.

• Inform the parents if rules or policies about behavior change.

• Stand behind the rules and policies of the school, and the classroom standards of individual teachers. Parents respect an administrator who stands firm. You must emphasize the intention to have a good climate in the school.

• Even though parents are concerned about their own child, they and their children share responsibility for supporting a positive climate for all children.

• When rules, standards, and punishments are openly discussed among parents, teachers, and students, there will be greater acceptance of the "fairness" of school policies.

7.62 Helping Parents Seek Outside Resources

• You should be familiar with other resources for helping parents and children cope with problems (see Section 7.212 for a list of such agencies).

• Have a contact in each agency whom you can call when a problem arises. Parents who are directed to such resources are more likely to use them if they are referred to a "person whom you know."

• Admit that some problems are beyond the school's resources. While parents may insist that you "do something," the school cannot solve every problem.

• Be direct and candid when suggesting outside resources. Your confidence in making a recommendation will increase the parent's confidence in accepting it.

• The school psychologist or other resource personnel should be called upon for help in making referrals.

• Have parents give permission for information to pass between the school and an outside agency. Many parents are more comfortable if you remain involved.

7.63   How to Conduct Effective Parent Conferences

a. Have the conference in a comfortable place with adequate seating for adults. Provide ashtrays and coffee, as appropriate. Try to have a special place in your school for such conferences.

b. What do you want to accomplish in the conference? What do you wish to get across? What do you want the parents and child to do? When you have a plan, you can be more confident. You should alter your plan according to the circumstances you find.

c. Engage in relationship-building conversation before getting into the substance of the conference. Showing that you are interested in their situation and would like to help reduces their anxiety.

d. Attempt to reframe the child's behavior in a positive way. Point out the child's good points before pointing out problems. Parents need to know that you don't believe their child is "all bad."

e. Offer concrete examples of the problem(s). Vague or global generalizations tend to stimulate resistance and anxiety.

f. Listen to the parents. Give them opportunity to react to your comments. Solicit from them the problems they have at home (see Section 9.1 on Communications).

g. Recommend something *specific* for the parents to do. They will look to you for guidance. Determine their willingness and capability to do what you suggest.

h. Lay out "homework" for them. Commit yourself to doing something equally specific. You and the parents should be a "team" working on the problem.

i. Set a specific time and place for a follow-up meeting. If "homework" is to be done immediately, check by phone with them in a few days.

j. Thank the parents for attending the conference. Use the end of the conference for self-esteem building. Encourage and support the parents in what they need to do.

7.64 Dealing with Parental Fears, Guilt, and Sense of Inadequacy

• When parents are called "to the office" they may regress to feelings they had when they were children in similar circumstances. Such feelings may be expressed as resistance or anxiety. If parents with little education had problems in school as children, they may be hostile toward you as an authority figure.

• Share your own dilemmas as a parent. You may share similar problems that other parents have had, with proper safeguards for confidentiality.

• If parents have valid criticism of you or the school, your admission of mistakes will allow them to be more willing to admit errors.

• See Section 8.6 on dealing with personal problems of teachers, and Chapter 2 on conflict resolution. These sections are relevant to conflicts with parents.

• You are not a therapist, but this doesn't diminish your responsibility to be helpful. Your counsel can be specific and practical, and still have enormous value.

• You need to have things for parents to do. Guilt and anxiety are alleviated when a person does something successful to solve a problem. Doing something positive reduces feelings of inadequacy.

7.7 USING COMMUNITY RESOURCES

You are not alone! Schools can't solve every problem that parents or children have. But the school can bring to bear the resources that are needed to solve problems. Making use of such resources will make your work more effective.

7.71 How Various Agencies Can Help the School

Case Example: Johnny, a second grader, had been a behavior problem since he entered school. Coming from a single-parent family, his behavior had been attributed to poor parental control. When the new principal referred him to a local diagnostic clinic, it was discovered that Johnny had a remediable brain disorder. He was referred to a neurologist for more extensive work. A program of medication, behavior modification and special repatterning exercises soon reduced his problems and improved his academic performance.

Case Example: Sean had been a good student until recently, in third grade, when he stopped working and became a behavior problem. The teacher had tried to get the parents to school, but had no success. Through another parent who was concerned about Sean, the principal found out that Sean's parents were divorcing. He contacted Sean's mother and insisted that she come to see him. In a long, tear-filled conference, he found out how embarrassed and upset Sean's mother was about her divorce. He arranged for counseling for her at a nearby Family Service Agency. Within several weeks, Sean's behavior and academic performance improved, as his mother made a better adjustment to her situation.

Case Example: Danny, a second grader, missed school often, and when he did come looked downtrodden and very withdrawn. He was referred to the school psychologist, who was told by Danny that his stepfather often beat him. He showed the psychologist bruises on his back as proof. The principal and the psychologist met with the parents, who denied abusing Danny, but were tense and vague about the causes of the bruises and gave ambiguous reasons for his absences. In the weeks following the meeting the pattern did not change, but Danny reported more instances of beatings. The principal contacted the Children's Protective Division of the County Welfare Department, and discussed the situation with them. A case worker visited the home, and was concerned about the conditions he found. Subsequently, Danny was removed from the home and placed in a temporary foster home. The parents were ordered by the court into counseling, which resulted in the stepfather leaving the home. Danny was returned to his mother, and there was no further evidence of abuse.

7.72 Checklist of Agencies Concerned with Children's Welfare

____Catholic Social Service

____Public health department, children's services

____Children's Home Society, for placement or adoption

____Churches and church-related welfare projects (contact local council of churches)

____Family Service Association

____Other counseling centers

____Drug abuse programs

____The Special Services Department of your local or county district

____Service clubs (Elks, Kiwanis, Lions, etc.) who may have projects dealing with children

____County Mental Health Department, and special programs

____Juvenile Probation Department

____Diagnostic facilities for children

___Big Brother or Sister organizations
___Juvenile officers, local police or sheriff's departments
___Local or County Recreation Departments
___Salvation Army
___Senior Citizens; Foster Grandparent programs
___County Social Welfare Department, children's services
___Local United Way Office (information)
___Volunteers Bureau
___YMCA, YWCA

7.8 DEALING WITH PRESSURE GROUPS

As a "public official," you have a constituency—the parents of your school. Your constituency is composed of people with varying opinions and attitudes, who may band together to press for changes that they value. How to deal with them is the focus of this section.

7.81 Types of Pressure Groups

Philosophical Purists: Who hold strongly to one educational point of view; i.e., basic fundamentals, open classrooms, humanistic education.

School Politicians: Whose basic motive is to increase their influence over school affairs in general.

Minority Advocates: Who believe that the school has a negative effect on minority children, and that they know what you should be doing.

Thrifty Citizens: Who "know" how the schools are wasting tax dollars, and want to make the schools more accountable.

Personal Critics: Who take a dislike to a teacher or administrator for actual or inferred harm he or she is doing to children.

7.82 Creating a Place Where Pressure Groups Can Be Heard

Pressure groups cannot be disregarded, for they represent a constituency that should be heard. They may have ideas that are usable. They may be able to bring about events that will make your job more difficult.

When an irresistible force meets an immovable object, friction and heat result. You should not be that "immovable object." Being receptive to pressure groups diminishes heat.

Often pressure groups are amorphous collections of people, with no organizational structure. It's difficult, under this circumstance, to know with whom you are dealing. A parent who is well known and active in the community can become a pressure group of one member.

(Chapter 4 on Conflict Resolution, Chapter 9 on Communication, Chapter 2 on Problem Solving, and other sections of this Handbook have material relevant to dealing with pressure groups.)

Keep the following issues in mind when planning to deal with pressure groups:

• Keep an open-door policy. Be willing to discuss school issues with any concerned citizen.

• Attempt to clarify the constituency of those who say they are spokesmen for others.

• Use surveys to clarify the opinions of the parents at your school (see Section 7.3 on surveys and questionnaires).

• Be willing to arrange meetings and invite a cross-section of parents to attend.

• Have information available about the issues that pressure groups are raising.

• Keep notes of private meetings when highly volatile issues are being discussed with people who may, themselves, be volatile.

• Clarify your own limits and the limits of outside intervention in your school.

• Keep your central office informed of organized attempts to influence the school's policies.

7.83 Keeping Power and Sharing Power

The main goal of pressure groups is to influence school policies. Pressure groups, by their very nature, are making a bid for power. Such a bid has an impact on your authority, and on that of your staff (see Chapter 8 on Handling Stress).

The central problem is how to work with pressure groups so as to preserve the integrity of the school and people who work in it, and at the same time evaluate issues accurately and sincerely.

Power is related to roles. As administrator you have certain kinds of authority, just as your teachers have authority relative to their roles. How power is kept and shared is a problem in role clarification and role change (see Chapter 10 on Role Clarification).

7.84 Organizing Meetings to Defuse Conflicts

When pressure groups become public, the issues and conflicts raised by them usually must be dealt with in public meetings. If the conflicts are intense, there is a tendency to avoid public confrontations; but often confrontation cannot be avoided. (See Chapters 5, 9, and 2 on Conflict Resolution, Communications, and Problem Solving.)

7.85   When to Involve Superiors

It's no fun to be embroiled in conflict. Public conflict is ordinarily considered to be "politics," and schools have attempted to avoid being political. This is becoming increasingly difficult in many areas.

As a local school administrator, you have limited capability to contain conflicts that arise from pressure groups, and may need to turn to your central office. This, of course, cannot happen every time a parent complains. But there are situations in which it would be wise to involve your superiors:

1. When issues are raised in your school that could have implications for other schools in your district.
2. When conflict surrounds policies that arise from board or district decisions, but are being addressed to you.
3. When you agree with the critics, but feel required to defend district policies.
4. When people of substantial influence in your community have become (or are likely to become) school adversaries.

7.9   DEVELOPING PARENTS' SUPPORT FOR SCHOOLS

In order for parents to become a useful resource for the school, your interest in and ability to organize them is necessary. You have to know what you want from parents.

7.91   Making PTA More Effective

The PTA at Carter School had become a joke. They sponsored one major fund-raising event each year (a potluck supper or playday), and collected dues. The monthly meetings were caricatures, in which lengthy formal reports about minor issues were presented. If more than the officers showed up, it was a "big" meeting. The teachers needed things, but didn't have the time to explore community resources. When asked if the PTA could help, they laughed, "They've never done anything." Program consultants, who were working with the staff, asked the administrator to call a meeting of the PTA Executive Committee, to ask them if they really wanted to help the school. They affirmed their willingness, but said that they didn't know what to do. The program consultants suggested that they might survey the staff to find out what the staff needed, and determine what the PTA could do. A survey was completed that identified things the staff wanted from the PTA, and two staff members were selected, voluntarily, to work with the organization. The Executive Committee made a preliminary determination of materials and people that could be obtained from the community, and asked other parents to take responsibility for parts of the program. A program for the year was organized, and, with greater parent involvement and staff attendance at meetings, was put into operation. A year later the staff held an "appreciation dinner" for the PTA.

• If the PTA is moribund, the above is one way to get parents started.

• When the PTA is isolated from real needs and concerns of the staff, the organization will diminish into irrelevance.

• The regional or national offices of the PTA can provide ideas and materials that will give you ideas to energize your group.

• Start with what you have. If the functioning PTA is only a small group, begin with programs they can accomplish.

• Staff participation is necessary if the PTA is to be a real resource. If strong leadership in the organization is missing, you may need to fill the vacuum.

7.92   How to Set Up a Parent Support Group if There's No PTA

A. Familiarize yourself with what PTA-type groups do. Write to regional or national PTA offices for information. Contact other administrators who have such groups in their schools.

B. Have material on hand and prepare a list of possible activities for such a group.

C. Contact a small group of interested parents and arrange a meeting at school or at one of their homes.

D. Organize a small group of parents at the meeting to work as a coordinating group. Ask them to assess whether parents are interested in such a group. Will it go? Remember that if only five percent of the parents were to become active, a lot could be done for the school.

E. Plan further meetings, with parents inducting others into the core group until there are enough (including yourself and some teachers) to fill the following subcommittee activities:

1. *Organization Committee:* by-laws, conditions of membership, officers, meetings, purposes.
2. *Finance Committee:* funding, budget, dues, fund raising, how money is to be used.
3. *Parent-Teacher Relations Committee:* how will teachers be involved? What interaction will occur between teachers and parents?
4. *Program Committee:* what will the new organization do? When, where, and how?

F. Complete planning for the organization, including name.

G. Plan the first activity, which should be designed to get a large number of parents to attend, i.e., carnival, potluck supper, back to school night.

H. Have materials, including membership applications, available at this event.

I. Publicize new organization through newsletter, letters to parents, and other devices.

J. Have children involved in the publicity.

K. Call an organizational meeting that can ratify plans, elect officers, and place the new organization on a firm footing.

7.93   Getting Out the Vote: Bond Issues and Elections

In recent years, school districts across the country have found it increasingly difficult to get public support for bonding and tax overrides. School boards have become politicized around issues of financial support for schools.

Many districts are marshaling internal resources for the political struggle which often arises from public resistance. As a building administrator, you may be called on by your central office administrators to help in "getting out the vote." Many administrators find this function to be confusing and stressful. Some fear that the role of public advocate will compromise their role as educator. Some fear that people will see them as a lobbyist for resources that accrue to their personal benefit.

Whether or not you can act in a positive way in these matters will depend on your relationship to the parents. If you have done the things that have been suggested in this chapter, you will be able to function effectively.

• If a pattern of good communication between school and parents has existed, conveying information about school financing elections will be normal and appropriate.

• If you have gained the respect of parents because you have been helpful, direct, honest, and an effective leader, they will be influenced by your opinions.

• If you have a supportive parent organization, they will be inclined to back you up when school matters become public issues.

• If parents have become attached to the school because of classes, meetings, and special events that have been useful to them, they will be motivated to come to informational meetings about such issues.

• If an attitude of willingness to help the school exists, then parents will be more likely to extend themselves into the voting booth.

• If you can show parents how public issues that concern the school have a direct effect on their child, it will bring home the importance of their support.

8

How to Handle Stress and Foster Personal Growth

Your job as a school administrator is one of the most stressful positions. You have to deal with demands and complaints from widely divergent types of people. Parents, teachers, children, and other administrators all try to influence you to act in certain ways. As stress increases, you will experience increased irritability, depression, headache or backache, lethargy, and frequent thoughts of getting away from it all. If you are lucky and haven't experienced these signs of acute stress, you still should know what to do in order to avoid such symptoms and how to deal creatively with the inevitable pressures of your job. Moreover, how you deal with stress affects teachers' morale and childrens' learning.

8.1 HOW LOW SELF-ESTEEM INCREASES STRESS

How you regard yourself has a direct effect on the way you bear up under pressure. If you feel isolated, not appreciated for your individuality, without power to change things, and without a sense of how to act or where to go—then almost any demands and minor inconveniences will be stressful.

8.11 Feeling Isolated—Lack of Connectiveness

Since the school administrator is usually one of a kind at a school, and set off from his peers, he or she will often feel isolated. There are limited opportunities for sharing problems with fellow administrators who, because of similar situations and backgrounds, might be most understanding.

Expressing your own tensions with your school's staff is often difficult because of fear of losing authority through being too personal. There is often the desire to avoid being closer to some staff members and contributing to staff dissension. These fears create tension by hindering the natural inclination to be attracted to some people rather than others because of similarity of background, experiences, philosophy, etc.

Think of all the people a school principal has to relate to:

- Teachers
- Resource Staff
- Parents
- Community resource people
- Aides
- Children
- Fellow administrators
- District personnel
- Secretaries
- School nurse

So many roles and agendas! Contacts are often brief and time pressures are high. It is difficult to establish any feelings of intimacy or connectiveness.

What can be done:

(See Chapter 6 on Self-Esteem.)
- Share your feelings, not just policies, with staff.

One newly appointed principal of a rural elementary school had difficulty being accepted. He knew that much was going on behind his back, but his efforts to establish rapport were met with polite superficiality by a well-entrenched staff. Many sleepless nights were spent in worrying because he liked the school. Only when he began to share his joy and excitement about hunting and fishing, which had attracted him to that locale, and his frustration about a malfunctioning well, did the staff begin to open up.

Mutual and appropriate self-disclosure between people reduces fear and suspicion and lessens the need to spend energy creating safe facades.

- Encourage situations where being oneself is accepted and is the norm. For example: parties, staff talent show for children and staff, and school sport days where principal and staff enter into the games.
- De-centralize decision making and authority, making it easier to share oneself. Staff members' fears of exposure to a powerful authority figure will be reduced

8.12 The Unexpressed Self—Lack of Uniqueness

Think back to the time when someone sincerely appreciated something that was a unique expression of you, e.g., a photograph you took, the way you expressed your ideas, etc. How do you feel? That experience of appreciation for your uniqueness is hard to come by when your administrator's role is constrained by policies and customs. To be sure, there are organizational demands that must be attended to; yet, at the same time, you are a person with unique human needs that don't disappear while you are at work. We all have needs for variety, for relaxation and laughter (tension release), for human contact on a personal level, for predictability and safety. To avoid dealing with these needs on the job is to create opportunity for tension and stress.

What can be done:

• Cultivate a rewarding life outside of school by engaging in activities and books that are not related to education. Find friends outside your profession. ⚹
• Evaluate the limits of policy and the apparent definitions of your role so that you find ways to express your own personality. For example, take on a teaching task, redecorate your office, etc.
• Share your innovative ideas with teachers and encourage brainstorming. Share your ideas as a regular part of problem solving (see section on Brainstorming).

8.13 Problems in Making Things Happen—Lack of Power

The paradox of power is one of the problems that can make a school administrator's job difficult. If you exercise too much power, the climate of a school can deteriorate. When you don't exercise power appropriately, the resulting ambiguity and confusion can create tension, and disrupt a healthy learning environment.

Finding the balance of power is made more difficult by the number of people who want to share the power. Also, there are those who avoid taking responsibility, while at the same time they want to influence decisions.

A feeling of powerlessness may arise from a school administrator's sense of being ill prepared for the complexity of the job. The administrator, often having little direct impact on children, is much more a facilitator of the harmony between groups. The satisfactions from facilitating are indirect and dependent upon the actions taken by others. It requires patience and keen observation to wait for and see the results of compromise, encouragement, and efforts to help others become more capable.

What can be done to increase a sense of power?

(See Chapter 6 on Self-Esteem.)

• Sharing power by distributing power to various groups, and freely accepting the role of facilitator. The administrator needs to see that he or she has the power to get other people to do things rather than doing things him or herself.

• Clarify goals and roles so that you know who is responsible for accomplishing things. In this way, people can be held accountable for their actions.

• Admit your own lack of knowledge when appropriate, and acknowledge your competence when present. Freely allow yourself to be a student, without feeling inadequate for not knowing something.

• Time spent in making others feel important will help them to be willing to listen to you and accept what you say.

8.14   Where Am I Going?—A Lack of Goals

The rapidity of change in our schools has increased the difficulty of finding stable roles in which a continuing sense of competence can be experienced. Moreover, styles of administration that served as models years ago are no longer appropriate. The practice in some districts to reassign the principals after four to five years in a school also hinders the acquisition of stable standards for appropriate behavior. The reassigned administrator often finds that the administrative styles that worked well at one school often do not work as well with a new staff and community. Furthermore, the new staffs are often hesitant to accept new norms, and communications are often distorted during such transitions.

What can an administrator do?

• Consider a time frame for promoting significant changes in terms of years rather than months, if a school district will allow such a time lapse to occur.

• Clarify your own values while at the same time acquiring knowledge about the staff's expectations. How can you clarify your values?

1. Keep a journal in which you write down ideas, feelings, directions (see book by Progoff[1]). The journal will allow unspoken ideas and vague feelings to be clarified and you will experience increased coherence in your own ideas.

2. Seek conversation with people who are willing to share ideas different

---

[1]Progoff, Ira; *At a Journal Workshop*. New York. Dialogue House Library, 1975.

from yours and who can challenge you. You can ask friends to play a devil's advocate role.

3. Accept and then express in writing or conversation your visions about education and how you'd like to further this vision. Don't immediately demand practicality, but view it in terms of underlying values that have gut-level meaning for you and are not to be dismissed as mere whimsy.

• Share your values with staff and parents and invite them to participate in a process of goal and role clarification (see chapters dealing with these subjects). It is useful to communicate early in your administration your long-range goals for the school. This gives staff a motivating vision as well as allowing those who cannot agree with this direction (and who might not be amenable to change) a chance to seek transfer or other employment.

8.2 HOW TO MANAGE YOUR TIME EFFECTIVELY

One of the most stressful issues that all administrators face is the pressure of too little time to accomplish too much work. We frantically try to cram, often in a helter-skelter way, the mountain of activities into the mole hill of time. Half-completed tasks only create more work and guilt. How can you get control of your time?

The first step is to really want to, and to believe that it is possible to use your time more effectively. The second step is to develop a plan to *gain* time. So, take time to review the following steps which will make a big difference when you follow them:

1. Take 30 minutes to think through and write down your goals and priorities. Start by thinking of long-range goals (what you want to be doing in five years), then short-range goals (six months to one year) in different areas such as work, recreation and hobbies, personal growth and education, relationships, spiritual and religious life.

2. Take the areas that have the highest priority and within each area rank the priority of the goals. Remember that some areas having high long-range priority may not necessarily be tops on a short-term basis.

3. Under each goal, brainstorm the activities that would lead you toward those goals.

4. Of these activities, select those that appeal to you as well as those that have to be done immediately.

5. From the above list, write down subtasks that you have to do, and put them on a "To Do" list, indicating their priority. For example, if you wish to reduce bickering among staff and raise staff cooperation within the next year, brainstorm activities such as an inservice communication course, school parties,

a minimum day for sharing new ideas, etc. From this list, you may decide that the inservice course needs to be started first. List subactivities that have to be done to bring this inservice about, such as check central office for status of inservice funds, talk to a fellow principal who had a similar course at his school, etc. These tasks go on your "To Do" list, which is kept in a place where you can refer to it easily.

6. Since unanticipated contingencies often shift priorities, you need to plan each day; take ten minutes to review goals and the "To Do" list for the week. This is time well spent. The best time for such planning is early morning or evening.

7. Find hidden time in such moments as lunch times, waiting for an appointment, etc. Cutting down on low priority activities also frees time; thus it is important to select and to act on high priority tasks.

8. Increase your motiviation for a task by starting on top priority items that can be done quickly, such as a phone call, a memo, asking your secretary to send for a book, seeing a teacher at lunch, etc. Such activities will get you into the project and will stimulate interest in continuing, whereas waiting for large blocks of uninterrupted time will often kill a worthwhile project. Chip away at large projects to avoid feeling depressed about not starting necessary activities.

9. Avoid the unreasonable taskmaster of perfectionism. When new projects are started, mistakes will occur and can be learned from. It is necessary to consciously give yourself permission to grow through imperfection.

10. Delegate (as much as possible) tasks you don't like or that have low priority. If you have to do many onerous tasks, you'll waste time by delaying, forgetting, and straining.

11. Read Alan Lakein's book, *How to Get Control of Your Time and Your Life*, Signet, 1974.

8.3 HOW TO RELAX AND REDUCE STRESS

Mental strain and body tension are closely related. You cannot have one without the other. It is also true that you can reduce worries and mental strain by relaxing the muscles of the body. Relaxation also will increase your physical health by facilitating the flow of blood, which provides life-giving nutrients to cells and flushes away waste. Relaxation produces slow and regular brain waves (alpha waves). In this alpha state, people can often be open to unusual ideas which are the basis of creativity.

Therefore, when you learn how to relax you will:
- Worry less
- Increase your creativity

- Improve your physical health
- Help those around you to relax
- Increase work efficiency and quality of output.

Relaxation can be brought about in many different ways. Select those that fit you and allow the relaxation pause to become a life-giving habit. Frequent and short relaxation breaks are more effective than one long period. Here are some ways to relax:

1. *A pleasant place:* Create a pleasant, private place for yourself. Put flowers, tapestries, rugs, statuary, pictures, etc., in your office. A beautiful, harmonious setting improves relations and your disposition.

2. *Play:* Play with the children during your lunch break (when you can take time for lunch).

3. *Stretch:* Go outside and really stretch; open your mouth and yawn. With the increased oxygen will come renewed energy.

4. *Palming:* When your eyes ache, use palming to relieve the fatigue. In palming, you cover your eyes with your palms so no light comes through. Rest the bottom part of your hands on your cheek bones. Do not press so hard that you feel pressure on your eyes. Try to remember what black looks like and just see black. Then let your mind go to a place that is comfortable and relaxing, and see yourself at that place. Palm for two to three minutes.

5. *Total body relaxation:* There are different methods for using self-suggestions and imagery to relax the whole body. You will generally take about ten minutes in the beginning to get to a deep state of relaxation. With practice, you can learn how to relax within five seconds.

Three books give detailed explanations of relaxation methods:

C. Eugene Walker, *Learn to Relax: 13 Ways to Reduce Tension.* Prentice-Hall, Inc. 1975.

Samuels and Bennett, *The Well Body Book.* Random House/Bookworks, 1973.

Bruno Geba, *Breathe Away Your Tension.* Random House/Bookworks, 1973.

6. *Meditation:* There now is scientific evidence that meditation brings deep relaxation. You don't have to spend money for learning special mantras; just get into a relaxed posture and focus your mind on a neutral, reoccurring, somewhat monotonous stimulus, such as your breathing.

In his book, *The Relaxation Response* (William Morrow Company, 1975), Herbert Benson talks about the "relaxation response," which is a form of meditation.

8.4 HOW TO DEAL CREATIVELY WITH CRITICISM

Along with your position comes the likelihood that you will become the focus of criticism. Learning to deal with it will determine how comfortable you will be in your job.

8.41 Our Worst Enemy—Fear

Fear of being criticized is often worse than criticism. You may experience this fear as a reluctance to take necessary action or a persistent avoidance of a problem. Such avoidance will only lead to further misunderstanding and criticism.

8.42 Psychological Judo—Redirect Blame into Problem Solving

A person who has criticized you has energy that can be redirected if you can avoid feeling that you have to defend yourself. How can you do this?

1. Assert yourself by inquiring about the details of the other's criticism, in order to understand the critic's perspective. "What is it about this decision that bothers you?" Or, "Are you saying that my decision means that I am critical of the way you teach reading?"

2. Often the first criticism is a cover for other things that are bothering the person. You might ask, "I can see that you are unhappy about the way I talked to Mrs. Jones. Are there other things I've done that have disturbed you?"

3. Invite the other person to participate in the problem solving. For example, Mr. A., an elementary school principal, was criticized by his staff for not being present enough at school. Much of this criticism came to him indirectly via his secretary who had overheard staff gossip. At the next staff meeting, Mr. A. shared his concern about the demands on him that took him away from school and asked for reactions of his staff to his absences. Tentative complaints became stronger when Mr. A. fully listened without defense and inquired about details. Mr. A. then asked the staff to help him problem-solve the situation so that their needs as well as central office's demands were met. The resulting discussion brought about a clarification of roles, a change in priorities of certain activities, and a sharing of certain responsibilties among other staff.

4. Admit to shortcomings without self-castigation and "Yes, but . . ." statements which shift the responsibility (and blame) to another person. Showing that one can still be O.K. and make mistakes is enormously stress-reducing for you and your school. A simple, "Yes, I made a mistake," without apologies, serves to reduce staff defensiveness and criticism.

5. At the same time that you are willing to recognize shortcomings, also set limits. Admit that you cannot be everywhere at once and therefore the problem does involve others' responsibilities.

6. An angry person needs to be listened to before he can attend to any of your suggestions or point of view. Paraphrase what he says and affirm that his feelings are important (see Chapter 9 on Communication).

7. Give yourself time to review the criticism before responding. Let the person know you have heard him through paraphrasing, and set a time to respond. This is particularly important if your feelings are so intense that you cannot trust your response at the moment. Later, review what got you so "hooked" by the other person's statements.

8.5   WHEN THE MANAGER BECOMES A MIDDLE MANAGER—WORKING WITH SUPERIORS

Being a subordinate often requires as much skill as being a boss. Here are some hints to help you deal with that part of your job.

8.51   Check Messages—Both Formal and Informal

Our school systems generate countless rumors, especially during times of tight money and staff firings. You need to be a model of good communication, by checking rumors and clarifying roles and responsibilities.

8.52   How to be a Member of a Team

Sometimes administrators are leary of being cajoled into "being a member of the team." They fear that such pressure is designed to get them to give in and agree so that harmony exists. Agreeing for harmony's sake alone lowers not only one's own self-esteem, but also the effectiveness of the team. Being a team member *does* mean:

1. You are willing to listen to other members and take time to indicate that you have heard (see Chapter 9 on Communication).

2. You express your likes and dislikes clearly, directly, and appropriately, thus providing important information for team problem solving. Inappropriate solutions often result when you hold back criticism for the sake of harmony.

District A was proposing to institute year-round schooling in order to make more effective use of facilities and reduce the stress of increased population and inadequate space. A recent bond election had failed. Bill M., a principal of a school with a large minority population, felt uncomfortable about his superintendent's pressure to be a spokesman for the proposal. Bill already knew from parents that they would object strongly, but he agreed to "sell" the idea rather than pushing for community surveys and support. He found, however, that going along with the superintendent's suggestion created heated discussions and divisions at his school. Eventually the school district had to abandon the plan because of community pressure, and Bill, finding his position constantly under parental attack, was transferred to another school.

3. Help your school know the central office administrators by asking them into your school to talk with staff. This will increase your staff's feeling that these administrators value the staff's contribution and will listen to their problems.

4. Give credit to team members' ideas. You will enhance others' self-esteem and the feeling of team connectiveness.

8.53   Getting What You Want and Need—Being Assertive

Many middle managers are cowed by persons in higher positions. They feel they do not have the right to ask for things they need. Superiors will sometimes present priorities as fixed and not open to negotiation. But you don't have to go along with the game. You have every right to ask just as they have the right to refuse. "Fixed" priorities have been known to shift under the weight of persuasive arguments.

For example, Mary K.'s school was particularly concerned about playground safety and wanted additional soft material put under the swings and climbing equipment. When the principal approached the central office, she was told there were limited funds and her request had low priority. Mary K., however, pointed out that community support was particularly important for the forthcoming bond election, and much of the concern for safety was coming from the parents. Mary got the money. She had done two important things:

1. She was assertive in pursuing her request and was not turned away by the first rebuff.

2. She had couched her request in terms of central office needs. Principals who seem to be the most effective are those who ask for more than they can possibly get, but they get something by repeated asking. If you are willing to do this, you, of course, must be willing to be turned down a majority of the time. There has been an increased interest recently in "assertiveness training." Two books that deal with this and provide exercises for the reader are:

Fensterheim, Herbert and Baer, Jean, *Don't Say Yes When You Want to Say No.* New York, Dell Publishing Company, 1975.

Smith, Manuel J., *When I Say No, I Feel Guilty.* New York, Dial Press, 1975.

8.54   Knowing When to Quit and Move On

Most of us, from time to time, have struggled with the idea of quitting our job. There are times when stress increases beyond what we think is tolerable, and our attempts to alter the situation have produced little or no results. What can you do at this point?

1. Make it O.K. to quit; leaving is not "wrong" or even an indication of failure. Quite possibly, growth in your awareness and changing values make a previously tolerable situation intolerable. Events, not of your making, have brought you to consider whether or not to quit.

2. Make your decision not only on the basis of job availability, but also on a careful consideration of your personal goals—what you want to be doing in five to ten years.

3. Talk over your struggle with friends who are good listeners—and who are not in the district. Getting a different viewpoint can help clarify your values and goals.

8.6   DEALING WITH PERSONAL PROBLEMS OF STAFF

Whether you like it or not, you will have to listen to or deal with the personal problems of some staff members. There are times when a staff member's personal problems are obviously hindering his or her performance. Unless dealt with, such a situation can be a continuing source of stress to you and to your staff, not to mention the children.

Elaboration of some of the ideas discussed below can be found in Chapter 9 on Communication, and Chapter 4 on Conflict Resolution.

8.61   Some Simple Counseling Techniques

Whenever a staff member shares his feelings of stress with you, you are serving as a counselor. To avoid this because you feel that you are not a therapist, would deny your potential to help relieve stress and assist in problem solving. A person seeking help will sometimes be open to suggestions that he or she seek professional help.

If you are placed in and accept a temporary counseling role, what can you do?

8.611   Listen

The experience of being listened to without judgment is stress reducing. Hold back offering suggestions or your own point of view. Attempt to understand the other's view of his situation. Paraphrasing his ideas and feelings will help the staff member to feel understood (see Chapter 9 on Communication). A person will be resistant to any further exploration until he can fully express his feelings and feel he is accepted.

8.612   Clarify alternatives

Stress is increased when a person feels stuck or helpless, and believes that only unpleasant alternatives and consequences are possible. You can help a person explore alternatives by such questions as:

"Have you thought of . . . ?"
"How do you know that . . . will not work?"
"How do you know that Mr. A. will not accept you if you tell him how you feel?"
"Would you be open to brainstorming some alternatives for you?"

You will be most helpful when you encourage others to explore alternatives and make their own decisions, rather than strongly suggesting a particular course of action.

8.613   Thinking through responsibilities

Each of us is ultimately responsible for our feelings, our actions, and thus for solving our own problems. To blame others for our condition is to give away our power to make decisions, for the questionable gain of feeling somewhat less guilty. You can help by focusing the person's attention on what *he* can do and away from how awful someone else is. Such statements as "What choices are open to you?", "You seem to be making the other person responsible for your feelings.", "I can hear you saying you are very angry at_____," "Have you thought of what you can do about this situation?" help the person to see that although he may affect another person's feelings, he is not responsible for other's feelings. (See Chapter 9 on Communication for elaboration.)

We frequently burden ourselves with worries that are not our concern, including trying to solve other people's problems. You can help by questioning how clear the staff member is about his responsibility.

8.614   The importance of being accepted

Often the staff member who shares his problems with you is really asking to be accepted by you.

Case Example: Julie, C., a recently hired fourth grade teacher, asked if she could speak with Mr. F., her principal. In his office, she burst into tears about her difficulties with an older teacher, a long-time staff member at the school. This teacher had, according to Julie, made some very paternalistic remarks about Julie's unruly class. Julie felt these remarks were unfair because the other teacher ignored the difficulties of starting a highly individualized program.

Mr. F. recognized the anger underneath Julie's tears and indicated he understood the difficulties of change. Julie's anger toward the other began to lessen after Mr. F. described his own struggles as a teacher to adopt a new program. He asked Julie to seek his help if she had any problems with the program. Mr. F.'s sharing of himself and offer of help showed acceptance of Julie, which she needed. He and Julie also discussed how she could listen to the older teacher's complaints without making either herself or the teacher wrong.

8.615   Not feeling you have to help

When someone is put in the "helper" role we have to be aware of the dangers of that position. An excessive desire to be a successful helper can lead to:

- Pressuring the other to take a course of action we feel is best.
- Subtle seeking of "thank you's" and other signs of appreciation.
- Getting angry if the other rejects our advice—"After all, I'm only trying to help!"
- Taking over the other's responsibility to solve his own problem.

8.62   When and How to Advise a Teacher to Seek Professional Help

There are times to suggest that a staff member seek professional help. When are these times?

1. When the above suggestions do not work!

2. When the person's problems are seriously hindering his or her performance.

3. When you are seriously concerned that the person's behavior indicates increasing stress over a long period of time.

When approaching the teacher:

1. Recognize that the suggestion itself may be anxiety-producing. Emphasize that the person's positive qualities are being stifled by this stress.

2. Specify what you have seen that concerns you.

3. Point out that stress symptoms are signals that a problem exists that needs attention. Not to seek the best resources available is foolish and a sign that we are avoiding the problem.

4. Give specific suggestions, such as name of several local therapists.

5. Make clear that seeking help is not a sign of weakness or bad character, but rather a rational, logical and sensible step that recognizes both our limitations and the possibility of growth and change.

8.63   Isolating Personal Problems from Organizational Needs

Jan's constant chatter was a source of amusement for those who didn't have to work with her, but exasperated those on the school reading committee. The chairman's attempts to focus on business hardly stifled the descriptions of Jan's classroom woes and chatter about her garden. When the principal finally confronted Jan about this she at first defended her actions, but then confessed her difficulty in controlling her talking. She added, "I guess I feel lonely, and I'm afraid I'm being ignored." The principal pointed out how her inability to be silent tended to interfere with the committee's work and that Jan had to set limits on herself or not participate. Jan sought professional help and did control her talking. She also found people listened to her more when she listened to them.

Staff members need to know when and how their personal behavior distracts others from working toward organizational goals. Sometimes what seem to be challenges to your authority are legitimate requests or criticisms. An open discussion of criticisms and a fostering of problem-solving orientation can help clarify which criticisms stem from a person's difficulty with authority.

Letting a person know what the limits and consequences are for his behavior can aid him in controlling himself so as not to interfere with necessary work.

8.7   PLANNING FOR PERSONAL AND PROFESSIONAL GROWTH

Personal change, like physical change, is a life-long experience. "Growth" means more than change. Growth implies that our change is positive, and expands our capabilities to handle stress in a wider range of situations—changes that enhance our self-esteem.

Our approach to self-esteem focuses on four conditions or ongoing experiences that enhance a person's self-confidence and positive liking for him or herself. (See Chapter 6 on Self-Esteem.)

Personal and professional growth can be viewed as increasing the degree to which all four conditions are present in one's life.

To help you assess your own needs and to focus on what particular conditions may be most lacking in your life, the questionnaire in Figure 8-1 is provided.

Rate each of the items below from 1 to 4 on the extent to which you are able to perform each behavior.

1 = hardly able to do this at all,
2 = sometimes able to do this, but I still strongly need to increase my capacity here.
3 = I can do this fairly often, but feel I could improve in this area.
4 = I can do this often and in a manner I feel satisfied with.

AREA A: CONNECTIVENESS

A sense of belonging, closeness, or affection to people, groups, and activities that are important to me.

_____1. I am able to ask for help or can ask someone for something I need without feeling inadequate or guilty.
_____2. When I'm with another person, I feel "fully there" without finding my thoughts drifting away to other things.
_____3. When I talk to others, my words and voice match how I feel.
_____4. I take an active part in a group or groups and enjoy being involved.
_____5. When I like someone, I can show him directly how I feel.
_____6. I can be aware of how my body feels, what parts are tense, when I need a rest, etc., and seriously try to follow what my body tells me it needs.

AREA B: UNIQUENESS

A sense of how my "differentness" from others is important and worthwhile so that I engage in activities that affirm the differentness.

_____1. I can express my ideas without waiting to hear what other people think.
_____2. I can "go with" my feelings and let myself experience them as an important part of me without getting stuck with or hanging on to any particular feelings.
_____3. I take time to show my own taste and interests in such things as

---

FIGURE 8-1

how I decorate my office, how I dress, and how I express myself. The expression of myself in these areas is more important than what others will think of me.

_____4. There are times I choose to be alone, to withdraw from others and be by myself—resting, loafing, or doing something I enjoy. At these times I do not feel I have to be "productive."

_____5. I take time to enjoy my imagination and creativeness.

_____6. I can share my point of view even when others differ with me

AREA C: POWER

A sense that I have the resources, capabilities, and opportunities to exercise control over my life, and can effect changes in my immediate environment.

_____1. I can handle a great deal of pressure without stomach upset, headaches, etc.

_____2. I am able to set firm and clear limits for myself and others without trying to make either myself or the other person guilty.

_____3. I can express my feelings appropriately without feeling I'm losing control.

_____4. I seek and enjoy being in charge of and responsible for projects and activities.

_____5. I can make decisions without excessive delay or stress.

_____6. I can take risks in new situations and find them challenging and exciting.

AREA D: MODELS

A sense of knowing and valuing my goals, values, and ideals; knowing how to act appropriately in many situations.

_____1. I have several important goals which guide what I do with my life.

_____2. I make attempts to clarify what my superiors expect of me and what constitutes a "good job."

_____3. I am developing a philosophy of life that is helpful in guiding me through periods of confusion and ambiguity.

_____4. I am finding that the activities I engage in increase my feeling that my life has meaning and purpose.

_____5. I can share my values with those who are close to me in a manner that is satisfying to me even though they may not have the same values.

_____6. I try to put myself into experiences that I feel would challenge, deepen, and enrich my philosophy of life.

FIGURE 8-1 (continued)

After you have completed the questionnaire, determine the extent to which you need to consciously work toward your personal and professional growth. Sources to consider in furthering your growth are:

1. Taking time to read some books that challenge you and add to your self-knowledge.

2. Investigate university extension classes that would allow you to not only gather information, but to experience yourself.

3. Look at the various "personal growth centers" in your area and consider taking some programs that are led by people who are established in the community and have a good reputation as teachers.

4. Allow time just to be with yourself on walks, writing in a journal, expressing yourself in art, etc.

5. If one of your friends has changed positively, ask what he did or what happened. Maybe what he did would fit for you.

6. Finally, realize that growth is a life-long task, and *be patient*.

9

Effective Communication
– Loud and Clear

You cannot *not* communicate. Every verbal or non-verbal interaction with someone is communication. Thus "communication" is a broad area. This chapter will emphasize what you as an administrator can do to establish procedures in your school that will nourish effective communication.

What is *effective* communication?

1. It is *direct:* People complain only to people who can do something about a disagreement or complaint. "Backbiting" is avoided.

2. It is *complete:* People are sensitive to what others need to know and include not only information about events, but also information about their internal facts, such as personal feelings and attitudes.

3. It is *relevant:* People avoid shifting topics to confuse and distract. People are sensitive to listeners' needs and situational constraints, e.g., time limits.

4. It is *congruent:* The speaker's words fit with voice tone and non-verbal messages. Angry words spoken from a smiling face lead to listeners' confusion.

9.1 PRINCIPLES OF EFFECTIVE COMMUNICATION

What follows is a brief overview of some of the principles of communication that are relevant to your job.

9.11 Personal Factors That Influence Communication

The staff of Kensworth Elementary School eagerly awaited their first meeting with their new principal, John W. They were very curious about him because he had been hired from outside the district. At the first staff meeting, many teachers were impressed with John's logical and precise mind. His phrases were like college outlines—complete, enumerated, and to the point. Others, however, felt intimidated by the flood of facts and the lack of feeling in John's voice. Moreover, many teachers soon found, to their discomfort, that in one-to-one conversations, John seldom looked at them while speaking or listening.

Two weeks later, at the school party for the new principal, many teachers were surprised to see John transformed: he spoke with feeling, and his sparkling eyes looked into theirs. One of the teachers, friendly with John, told John how surprised he was with these two widely different communication styles. Although John knew about these two aspects of himself, he had not been aware of the staff's reactions.

That evening, when John shared this experience with his wife, she pointed out how much emphasis his family had placed on being logical, without sharing feelings. John then recalled how he had often been punished by his father, for crying or showing anger, by being sent to his room. The only place where feelings were permitted was at parties, where his father was able to express strong feelings under the influence of alcohol; the family accepted such an excuse. John also realized that not looking at people helped him to think clearly; his feelings became stronger when he looked directly at people.

John decided to change his communication style at school and attended communication classes. Both he and his staff found that they understood each other better when John was able to look directly at the speaker and when he described his feelings and showed them in his voice.

Two main personality factors strongly affect communication style:

- The level of a person's self-esteem.
- Learned styles of coping with stress when self-esteem is threatened.

A person with high self-esteem, even under stress, will show the following communication characteristics:

1. *Congruent messages:* The voice tone, gestures, and words all fit together.

2. *Awareness of communication style:* The person is aware of his communication and does the following:

- He apologizes for a mistake and not for his existence.
- When there is a need to criticize, he evaluates the action and not the person.

Constructive suggestions are given and there is a readiness to listen to the other's point of view.

- In talking about intellectual things, he uses precise words, but still shows feeling.
- He realizes the need to change topics, yet he can make the other person aware that he is doing this. He can ask directly for things, without beating around the bush.

3. *The communication is "whole":* The person's face, thoughts, feelings, gestures, posture, are all congruently involved in communicating.

As an administrator, you need to:

- Be aware of your communication style; ask for feedback.
- Create conditions in your school that support growth of staff in self-esteem (see Chapter 6 on Self-Esteem).

9.12 Interpersonal Factors That Influence Communication

The quality of the relationship you have with your staff and fellow administrators strongly influences how you communicate and what you communicate about. Your relationship is influenced by:

1. *Your previous history* with a person. If you have experienced a teacher only in his/her school role, your communication will be different than if you played golf with that person or belonged to the same religious group. If your first contact with this person was over a conflict, then you will have strong expectations of conflict in the future, and your communication will be guarded.

2. *Your own changing needs* influence who and how you meet people. Under stress you probably will seek those who are generally supportive and avoid those who are demanding. If you are feeling excited about a new idea, you might well gravitate to those who share this high energy and avoid those who like routine and predictability.

3. *Status differences* will affect how you and others relate, particularly in the case of those who may be sensitive to authority roles. Principals often feel pressured into "parent" roles by certain teachers whose actions call for nuturing support or strong limit setting. Some principals without awareness accept "parent" roles, *assuming* responsibility rather than *clarifying* responsibility.

If you wish to communicate effectively, build a positive relationship with a person. Some suggestions for doing this are:

- See them in a variety of contexts to help avoid stereotyping.
- Be aware that the qualities you see in another person are the result of *your* perception and not just "within" the other person.
- Use the techniques of Conflict Resolution (Chapter 4).

The following communication actions can also help to build positive relationship:

1. When you listen, cut down on your internal dialogue so you can hear.

2. Periodically paraphrase what the other is saying without using his exact words, but stating the essence of the message. For example: if the person says, "My classroom is chaotic; children can't settle down today," you can paraphrase by saying, "What I'm hearing is that you may be upset because the children will not focus on their school work; is that so?" Your question asks for confirmation of what you heard and what you assumed (that the person was upset).

3. Before automatically assuming that your understanding of another person's feelings are correct, check. Ask, "Are you feeling angry?" rather than "Why are you angry?" (Assuming without checking.)

4. When you need to be critical, be clear about:

a. What behavior you observed.

b. What is the source of your standard, e.g., school policy, group agreement, your observation of how this person affected others, or your own personal feelings.

c. State how you are upset in terms of your own feelings. Most judgments stem from your own personal feelings.

d. Change blame into problem solving. (See Chapter 4 on Conflict Resolution.)

9.13   Organizational Factors That Influence Communication

The following factors will make a significant impact on the quality of communication. By altering them, you can change how people communicate.

1. *Physical Arrangements:*

• Sitting behind a big desk will increase the feeling of formality and distance between two people.

• Discussion is easier in a circle than when people are seated in rows.

• When the kindergarten classrooms are physically separated from the rest of the building, the kindergarten teachers will find it more difficult to talk informally with the rest of the staff.

• Thin partitions between classrooms; open space with reverberating sound; stairs that creak; all affect noise level, and thus, ease of listening.

• A teacher's room that is unattractive, too small, or poorly ventilated, will discourage informal sharing of ideas and feelings.

2. *Variety of Communication Channels*

The greater the variety of possible channels, the easier it will be for people to communicate. Communication can occur through:

- Informal one-to-one conversations
- Formal (have an appointment) one-to-one conversations
- Bulletin boards
- Loud speaker
- Printed announcements and newsletters that are circulated
- Staff meetings, held regularly
- Meetings on special minimum days
- Informal groups outside school for work or play
- Parties
- Special school days, e.g., school olympics, costume days, etc.
- Inviting a staff member to your home
- Central office staff come to school; school staff go to central office
- Small gatherings in the teachers' room
- Team teaching: other special teams working together for a short period of time.

3. *Norms about Communication*

(See Chapter 5 on School Climate for further clarification of norms.) Norms are shared expectations about behavior. These shared expectations strongly affect communication in areas of:

- How important communication is: "We don't get together much; each person does his own thing."
- What is talked about and to whom: "Bilingual education is a red flag around here."
- How acceptable it is to express differences and disagreements: "You really get into a hassle if you try to teach in 'conventional' ways."
- What feelings can be shown and how: "They think you are weird if you say how you feel, especially if you are really angry."
- How trustworthy are words: "No one says what he means anyway."

9.2 ANALYZING COMMUNICATION PROBLEMS

There are a number of sections in this book that provide information and sample questions that relate to the area of communications: chapters on Parent Relations; Problem Solving; Role Clarification; School Climate. When you start to assess communication patterns and problems, you will automatically increase people's awareness of the importance of this area. When teachers complete questionnaires about communication, they become more aware of their own as well as other people's communication style. Such awareness can facilitate later discussion and problem solving and start to alter school climate.

9.21 How to Pinpoint Who Has Trouble Talking to Whom

1. Assess how parents feel about school communication. (See Chapter 7 on Parent-School Relationship.)

2. Assess which school function groups are having communication difficulty (see Section 10.321 for questionnaire). Then take those groups that have unmet needs and ask them, either in discussion or through a questionnaire, what information they need to have from the others.

9.22 How to Assess Which Communication Channels Are Not Effective

1. The questionnaire shown in Figure 9-1 is an example of what can be done. Adapt it to your own situation.

Assessing Communication Channels

Instructions: In order to help improve the effectiveness of different communication channels, we would like you to answer the following questions as thoughtfully as you can.

    A. Rate each of the following ways that we communicate in terms of these two scales:

    a. *Usage:*

        How frequently do you pay attention to or use this channel of communication?

            scale: 0 = Never   2 = Often

                      1 = Seldom   3 = A great deal

    b. *Satisfaction:*

        How rewarding and satisfying is your use of this channel?

            scale: 0 = Dislike a great deal

                      1 = Most of the time not rewarding

                      2 = Rewarding

                      3 = Enjoy a great deal

Rate each item by indicating the number of the rating under "usage" and "satisfaction" columns. If a channel is not present in your school, check N/A.

FIGURE 9-1

	Usage	Satisfaction	N/A
1. Newsletter	_____	_____	_____
2. Staff meetings	_____	_____	_____
3. Bulletin board	_____	_____	_____
4. Circulated announcements and memos	_____	_____	_____
5. Informal discussions in staff room	_____	_____	_____
6. Small planning or committee groups	_____	_____	_____
7. One-to-one talks with principal	_____	_____	_____
8. Team-teaching activities	_____	_____	_____
9. Contact staff outside of school hours	_____	_____	_____
10. Scheduled parent conferences	_____	_____	_____
11. Informal parent contacts (phone or face to face)	_____	_____	_____

    B. Indicate why you gave a low rating in either/or both usage and satisfaction. (0,1)

Item No.	Reason
_____	_____
	_____
_____	_____
	_____

FIGURE 9-1 *(continued)*

2. You can also assess the effectiveness of a particular channel by spontaneously asking staff to complete a questionnaire about information contained in a circulated memo, placed on the bulletin board or discussed in staff meetings, etc. In order to avoid activating their resistance and their memories of school quizzes, do not ask for names, and indicate that this is a survey of your administrative ability, and the effectiveness of the communication channels.

9.23 Assessing Communication Norms

(See Chapter 5 on School Climate.)

Ask people to describe their observation of communication behaviors in the school, and at the same time, ask if they think that people should or should not do that particular behavior.

Use the questionnaire in Figure 9-2 as a guide.

Communication Behavior

Instructions: Please indicate by checking the appropriate column for each of the behaviors listed below whether or not people should show that behavior at this school.

Also rate the frequency with which you have seen people show this behavior at school. Give a rating from 1 - 10.

    1 = Not at all
    5 = Moderately
    10 = A great deal

(Use other numbers, e.g., 2, 3, 4, etc., to indicate points in between 1, 5, and 10.)

	Should	Should Not	Frequency
1. Disagree in a meeting with the principal's statements that you feel are incorrect.	___	___	___
2. In a meeting, say that you are angry or upset at what is going on.	___	___	___
3. Push for new ideas, even if they are vague and unusual.	___	___	___
4. For the most part, keep your real thoughts and feelings to yourself.	___	___	___
5. In a meeting, if you are not clear about a point, ask questions, even if everyone else seems to understand.	___	___	___
6. Tell the playground teachers you don't like the way they are treating a child from your class.	___	___	___
7. Avoid disagreement and conflicts whenever possible.	___	___	___
8. Be critical of another teacher in a staff meeting.	___	___	___
9. Reveal close, intimate things about yourself only to close friends.	___	___	___
10. Avoid criticizing another person when that person is not present.	___	___	___

FIGURE 9-2

	Should	Should Not	Frequency
11. Complain about something only to those who can directly do something about the complaint.	_____	_____	_____
12. In order to be safe, check all new ideas out with your supervisor.	_____	_____	_____
13. Confront a person who has been talking behind your back.	_____	_____	_____
14. Tell another teacher specific things he or she is doing that upset you.	_____	_____	_____
15. Let your supervisor know specific things that he or she is doing that bother you.	_____	_____	_____
16. Stick to facts and logic and avoid getting emotional over issues.	_____	_____	_____
17. Walk away rather than engage in gossip about other teachers.	_____	_____	_____
18. When you like what someone has done, tell him directly.	_____	_____	_____
19. Avoid complaining to other teachers about a difficult child.	_____	_____	_____
20. Remain silent about your ideas when you are not on sure ground.	_____	_____	_____

FIGURE 9-2 (continued)

In analyzing the results, there are several interesting comparisons:

1. Items on which there are large splits in faculty markings in the "Should" or "Should Not" columns indicate differing values and can be areas for discussion.

2. When many people do not show desired communication, there are blocks to effective communication. For example, one such block would be fear of being criticized, believing that others would not have the same values. Group discussion of questionnaire results can help free these blocks.

9.3 DEVELOPING ONGOING COMMUNICATION PROCEDURES WITHIN THE SCHOOL

Before developing new procedures in your school, you need to have first analyzed the communication needs of your school as described in Section 9.2 above. Of particular importance is determining who needs to talk to whom about what. (See Section 9.21.)

9.31 How to Get Your Staff Interested in Communications

Although many staff sense that communication difficulties are the basis of many problems, they are either reluctant to face the issue or confused about how to start. You can increase their interest and focus their attention by the following activities:

1. Complete a communication survey which is followed by feedback of the results to the staff; use these results as a basis for plans to meet identified issues.

2. Increase the opportunity throughout the year for feedback. For example, near the end of three months, ask the staff to write down "what was most helpful in your work" and "what hindered you in your work." Then review the answers with the staff, paying attention to those items related to communication.

3. Ask the staff to give you feedback regarding your communications to them. Indicate what kind of feedback is most helpful to you. The following are guidelines to effective feedback:

• Feedback should be specific, e.g., "You talk very rapidly when you're excited and I have trouble following what you are saying."

• Feed back as soon after the event as possible.

• The person giving the feedback needs to ask if the other person (yourself) can hear feedback at this time. If you answer "no," indicate when you would be available.

• The person giving the feedback needs to be willing to listen to how you saw that situation and if necessary work out some change that is comfortable to both.

When you receive the same feedback from a number of different sources, you may need to change your behavior and plan steps for change. Realize at the same time that feedback about your behavior reflects the other person's biases and perspective as much as anything you are doing. You are always the decider in determining whether or not you should change in response to negative feedback.

4. Periodically ask staff to write down brief descriptions of helpful communications they have seen or experienced during the week. Include these descriptions (preserving anonymity if preferable) in the newsletter.

9.32 Increasing the Occasions for Effective Communication

You can increase information flow by increasing the attractiveness of different communication settings.

• Fix up the staff room so that people will want to use it for informal gatherings. New curtains, a tasteful rug, and comfortable furniture will affect how people feel in the room. Comfortable feelings facilitate effective communication.

• Frequently update the bulletin board and increase its attractiveness through cartoons, an unusual poster praising staff efforts, articles about classroom techniques, and a display of children's reactions. Develop a "communication committee" who would, as one of their duties, create new material for the bulletin board.

• Start a regular newsletter that meets the interests of staff and is not just an announcement of district and school policies. Make the newsletter artistically attractive.

• Help in the formation of small groups who, for a period of time, focus on a staff problem in order to propose new solutions to the total staff.

• Do special get-acquainted games at school parties that increase self-esteem. (See Chapter 6 on Self-Esteem.)

9.33 Facilitate New Communication Procedures

Besides providing for new and attractive situations for effective communication, you can institute the following procedures to increase accurate information flow.

• Discuss and agree on helpful communication norms for meetings. (See below.)

• Help train the staff in a problem-solving procedure (see Chapter 2 on Problem Solving).

• Develop regular procedures for obtaining participants' feedback about meetings and new programs.

• Discuss and clarify role expectations (see Chapter 10 on Role Clarity).

• Clarify with staff how and when to use the different decision-making methods of consensus, voting, and authoritative fiat. (See Chapter 2 on Problem Solving.)

9.4   HOW TO MAKE YOUR MEETINGS MORE EFFECTIVE

This section provides an outline of procedures for improving meetings at your school.

9.41   What to Do Before a Meeting—Structuring

A good part of the job of improving meetings occurs before the meeting! Taking time to prepare can have a marked impact on the meeting itself.

9.411   People

Determine who needs to be at the meeting and the best way of informing them about the time, place, and purposes of the meeting.

9.412   Place

The meeting place should be well ventilated (for non-smokers and comfort), contain comfortable and appropriate chairs and tables, and provide refreshment possibilities.

9.413   Time

The starting and ending time of the meeting should be clear to all participants.

✳ 9.414   Agenda

It is often helpful to have a committee elected by staff who can meet briefly with you to help decide which agenda items are most important.

Organizing the agenda:

There are three types of agenda items:

1. Information items
2. Discussion items
3. Planning or decision items

Before meeting:

1. Think through agenda items and separate according to above categories.
2. Set priorities—which items are most important at this meeting?
3. Allot time—how much time is allowed for each item?
4. Decide what kind of action will be required for each item.
5. Post agenda with the action that needs to be taken in a central location; encourage members to add items.
6. Check with those who have special reports to prepare to see if they have completed them.

9.415   A meeting to decide how to have meetings

It is essential at some time to call a meeting in which the faculty reaches agreement on the following items:

1. Standards for group discussion should be talked about and clarified. Such standards might include:

    a. People do not interrupt when another member is speaking.

    b. Speakers should be recognized by the chairperson before talking.

    c. Members should pay attention to each other rather than milling about, chatting with their neighbors, or falling asleep.

    d. When one or more persons begin to dominate the discussion, other members should feel free to comment on this.

    e. Directness. If a member is dissatisfied with the way the group is going, he should report his reactions directly to the group itself when it is in session. A member who expresses his dissatisfactions with the group outside of the meeting, should be asked to bring the matter up with the total group at a regular session.

    f. Survey. Any member may ask for a survey at any time. The requesting member states what he wants to know from the total group. Some other member then paraphrases or clarifies the topic until all are clear what they are being asked. Each person, in turn, briefly states his current position on the topic in two or three sentences. No one passes. They can indicate lack of information, or confusion, etc. *A survey is not a vote.* It does not bind the group or its members; it suspends any other activity.

2. Clarify the role of the meeting convener or chairperson. Some of the following ideas about a group convener serve as guidelines. Also consider the possibility that you may not be the best convener. Select a person from your faculty who has the facilitation skills described below.

Convening:

    a. A convener is a discussion leader. He should be a *facilitator,* not a *dominator.*

    b. Important tasks of the convener are:

        (1) Summarizing: Putting together in concise statements the areas of agreement and disagreement in the discussion.

        (2) Gatekeeping: Making sure that everyone has an opportunity to contribute, and that one or a few people do not dominate the discussion.

        (3) Asking questions: Insuring that all facets of an issue are brought to people's attention.

    c. The convener has a *legitimate authority* to conduct the meeting, and should be willing to exercise this authority. The authority includes:

        (1) Beginning and ending the meeting on time.

     ✓ (2) Insuring that the agenda is held to.
     ✓ (3) Determining relevancy in the discussion.
     ✓ (4) Setting guidelines for the discussion.
     ✓ (5) Demanding that the group decide any procedural matters that will help the discussion or clarify decisions that are made.
     ✓ (6) Requiring that responsibility for carrying out decisions is clarified.

d. The convener has the chief responsibility for being aware of the process of the meeting (how it is going). He should comment on the process from time to time, and must keep the group from becoming bogged down or confused. In order to accomplish this, the convener should:

    (1) Be very clear on all the agenda items.
    (2) Be aware of time.
    (3) Discourage redundancy.
    (4) Compliment the group when it has conducted itself efficiently.
    (5) Observe the group continuously. Do not get totally wrapped up in the substance of the discussion.
    (6) Insure that a secretary is taking notes of the discussion.
    (7) Check with the members after the meeting to see how they felt the meeting was conducted.

3. Continuing group agreements. Periodically, a group should review its agreements and discuss whether they are being kept. Agreements should not be considered sacred. An effective group will often change its prior agreements and plan actions to build commitments for new agreements. Most importantly, the group should be clear and explicit about what kinds of behaviors are expected.

9.42 What to Do During the Meeting

A lot goes on during meetings—more than the untrained eye can see. This section will help you be more aware of meeting behavior.

9.421 Clarify the agenda

1. Read the agenda through; ask members to propose additions.
2. Clarify (briefly) any item that members may not understand.
3. Leave time at the end of the agenda for new business.
4. Introduce guests.

9.422 Techniques to use during meetings

   ✓ 1. *Survey:* See description above (Section 9.415). This technique is useful when a few have dominated the discussion and you are not certain what the others are thinking. A survey is a useful way to check if you have consensus.

   ✓ 2. *"Accordion method":* When you have a large group (over eight), it is difficult to hold a discussion that involves everyone. When the issue concerns the entire group and everyone's input is important, then use this method:

a. Divide the group randomly (count off by the number of groups you'll need) into groups of from four to eight people.
b. Each group is to elect a chairperson and recorder.
c. Each group is to discuss, within a given time period, an issue on which they are to make some decisions. For example:
  • "List the three most important needs of the school."
  • "Brainstorm ideas for bringing parents and school closer together, and select the three most important and feasible ideas."
  • "Make a decision about which of the three proposed programs is most important, and list three important reasons why you made this decision."
d. Small groups return to larger group, their report is read, and their "product" (list) is posted for all to see.
e. Chairperson combines and integrates lists and then summarizes results.
f. The large group may then have a number of options.
  (1) Vote.
  (2) Refer information to subcommittee to seek more information and make recommendations at next meeting.
  (3) Hold a large-group discussion.
  (4) Break group down into the same small groups for further discussion and repeat the above process.

3. *Special committees:* Frequently an issue which seems to be limited and easily solvable turns out to be complicated; sufficient time has not been allotted to deal with this issue. You can then select a small committee consisting of interested and knowledgeable members whose task is to study the issue further and by next meeting (or other designated time) recommend a course of action. The responsibility and authority of this committee are discussed and agreed upon by the entire group. You should also indicate resources that would be available to this committee, such as:

• Your time
• Release time from teaching or other duties
• Outside consultants
• Money
• Books and other reference material

9.423   Being aware of what "group functions" are most appropriate

In order to facilitate meetings, you need to know which type of group functions you can fulfill most appropriately and which action is most effective at any given moment.

Here are two kinds of functions that have been identified in groups—*Task Functions and Maintenance Functions*[1]:

Task Functions are role behaviors that help the group to accomplish its agenda and goals, such as to make decisions and recommendations, to create a plan, etc. Maintenance Functions are those behaviors that facilitate positive relationships between group members, encourage friendly feelings, and create trust. Both sets of functions are needed, and, in a well-functioning group, are performed by various members. At any given moment, one set of functions may be more important than the other, and you can be sensitive to the need of the group for any particular function. Most groups require a balance between the two.

The following are descriptions of the behaviors in these two functions:

Task Functions

1. *Initiating:* Proposing tasks or goals; defining a group problem; suggesting a procedure or ideas for solving a problem.
2. *Information or opinion seeking:* Requesting facts; seeking relevant information about a group concern; asking for suggestions and ideas.
3. *Information or opinion giving:* Offering facts; providing relevant information about group concern; stating a belief; giving suggestions or ideas.
4. *Clarifying or elaborating:* Interpreting or reflecting ideas and suggestions; clearing up confusions; indicating alternatives and issues before the group; giving examples. Particularly important when lots of different ideas are being proposed without any one idea being elaborated.
5. *Summarizing:* Pulling together related ideas; restating suggestions after group has discussed them; offering a decision or conclusion for the group to accept or reject.
6. *Consensus testing:* Sending up trial ballons to see if group is nearing a conclusion; checking with group to see how much agreement has been reached.

Maintenance Functions

1. *Encouraging:* Being friendly, warm, and responsive to others; accepting others and their contributions; regarding others by giving them an opportunity for recognition.
2. *Expressing group feelings:* Sensing feeling, mood, relationships within the group; sharing your own feelings with other members.
3. *Harmonizing:* Attempting to reconcile disagreements; reducing tension through "pouring oil on troubled waters"; getting people to explore their differences.
4. *Compromising:* When your own idea or status is involved in a conflict, offering

---

[1]From Schmuck and Runkel, et. al., *Handbook of Organizational Development in Schools*, pp. 287-288, 1972.

to compromise your own position; admitting error; disciplining yourself to maintain group cohesion.

5. *Gate-keeping:* Attempting to keep communication channels open; facilitating the participation of others; suggesting procedures for sharing opportunity to discuss group problems.

9.43 Evaluating Meetings

The people who participate in a meeting can tell you whether it was a "good" one or not. They should be asked.

9.431 The importance of feedback

If you wish to improve your meetings, it is important to set aside time for participants to give feedback about their perceptions and feelings. Otherwise, you have no way of knowing if the procedures are working. Feedback is the single most essential ingredient for learning. It is thus useful to establish the expectation in your faculty that time will be given periodically to obtaining feedback.

9.432 Using questionnaires and surveys

After a meeting, short questionnaires can be given to obtain feedback. The results can then be conveyed to the faculty via newsletter, bulletin board, or the next meeting (if held soon after the feedback).

The questionnaire in Figure 9-3 is an example and involves the two main functions of a group—(1) to get the task done, and (2) to maintain and enhance positive relations among members.

Feedback Questionnaire

Directions: Circle the number on the scale that reflects your opinions of this meeting:

1. *Goals of this meeting*

Poor   1   2   3   4   5   Good

ambiguous;   clear;
not relevant.   relevant.

2. *Organization*

Poor   1   2   3   4   5   Good

chaotic or too rigid;   clear and made sense;
I felt confused or manipulated.   I did not feel pushed or
                                    restricted.

FIGURE 9-3

3. *Accomplishments*

Poor   1   2   3   4   5   Good

a waste of time;   good decisions;
poor or no decisions made.   I learned a lot;
                                  a rewarding meeting.

4. *Interest*

Poor   1   2   3   4   5   Good

bored;   excited;
wanted to leave.   interested and involved.

5. *Expression of feelings*

Poor   1   2   3   4   5   Good

feelings ignored;   feelings expressed as one's own;
negative feelings expressed by   concern and encouragement
name-calling and subtle put-   shown;
downs; no appreciation shown;   critical feelings expressed di-
no expressions of support;   rectly and recognized with at-
expressions of feelings criticized. tempts to work them through;
                                  support shown.

6. Did positive things happen to make this meeting a success?

yes _____ no _____ not clear _____

   If yes, what? _____

_____

_____

7. Did negative things happen that hindered the success of this meeting?

yes _____ no _____ not clear _____

   If yes, what? _____

_____

_____

FIGURE 9-3 *(continued)*

Other examples of surveys and questionnaires can be found in Schmuck, et. al. (1972). (See bibliography.)

9.44 Handling Special Problems

1. If one or two people dominate the discussion, ask if they could hold back for a while in order to get everyone's opinion. Call for a survey.

2. If time allocated to a particular agenda item is insufficient, you should call the group's attention to this and ask for group decision to:

• Spend a given number of minutes on this issue, or
• refer issues to special committee, or
• delay further discussion until next meeting.

3. If two people get angry at each other and start to call each other names and you sense that the two opposing viewpoints are shared by a number of other people, you can:

- Focus on the issues underlying the "personality characteristics" and ask each person to paraphrase the other's viewpoint, and, at the same time, recognize his feelings.
- If the issue involves only a small group of people or just two people, ask if they are willing to meet together with you in another meeting to discuss their concerns.
- Ask participants to describe their own feelings as feelings and not disguise the anger or upset that is their own with blaming or name-calling.
- Refer to Chapter 4 on Conflict Resolution.

4. If the group shows a lack of interest and is lethargic in discussions, you can:

- Share your observations and ask for feedback through a survey.
- Give out a feedback questionnaire at the end of the meeting and go over results with a special committee.
- Call a meeting to discuss how meetings can be made more effective (see Section 9.415).

5. If everyone is talking at the same time, or during the meeting people form their own subgroups, you can:

- Indicate the need for the group to focus on the problem and difficulty caused by these subgroups.
- Call a survey.
- Ask that people be recognized by the chairperson before speaking.
- Clarify norms in this area.

Remember: Successful meetings are essential to a positive school climate and a supportive atmosphere for teaching.

10

Role Clarification
– Getting It All
into Clear Focus

A well-functioning social system (your school) is always characterized by agreement among the members of that system (you and your staff) about who is to do what, how, and when. When your expectations of yourself (in terms of task performance) are the same as others' expectations of you, then you are experiencing a high degree of role clarity.

Many of the conflicts, problems, and ambiguities that occur within schools result from a lack of clarity about roles. Previous chapters on Conflict Resolution, Problem Solving, Planning, Dealing with Stress, etc., all help to resolve role confusion problems.

In this final chapter, the process for reducing ambiguity about roles is described. What roles are, and how to deal with change, are further considered.

10.1 IMPORTANCE OF ROLE CLARIFICATION

Defining roles requires clarifying expectations. They are always connected. You, as an administrator, define your role through clarifying what you believe others expect of you, and what you expect of yourself. As you change and grow, your expectations of your own performance change. When the personnel with whom you work change over a period of time, new expectations of you result. Roles are, therefore, not static; they need to be reviewed and changed periodically. Differing expectations result in disagreements about who's to do things.

10.11   Role Ambiguity Causes Personal Stress

John Alexander was administrator at Benjamin Elementary School for a year and a half. He had replaced Mrs. Forbish, who, during her ten years at Benjamin, had been quite motherly toward staff, students, and parents. Although few innovations occurred in the program during her tenure, her intimate and personal relationships engendered a feeling of loss when she left.

Alexander, was told by his superiors to "get things moving at Benjamin." By the end of his first year, proposals had been accepted to fund a new Title I project, an Early Childhood Education pilot program, and several special projects. Aides had been hired, and children had been moved to the school from minority areas of the city. Benjamin was a beehive of activity.

But, staff members were inundated with paper work and were surfeited with new teaching materials and aides. Cliques had formed around a number of issues. A group of teachers went to the superintendent complaining that Mr. Alexander was away from the school too much, did not provide educational leadership, was not available to discuss problems with teachers, and had a disinterested attitude toward their problems. Things came to a head when threats to initiate formal grievance procedures were made by staff.

Alexander, himself, felt harried and confused. His success in fulfilling his responsibilities was evident in the growth and change in the school's program. He didn't know why staff were so antagonistic. He wanted to avoid direct confrontation with them, for fear the teachers' organization would become involved. He had grown nervous and tense during the past few months.

Consultants were called in. A survey of staff attitudes revealed that a large percentage of the staff was quite supportive of Mr. Alexander, and the smaller part was antagonistic toward him. Most of the antagonistic group had been at the school during Mrs. Forbish's tenure. Their expectations of Alexander were colored by that experience.

Subsequently, several hours were spent in all-staff sessions in which expectations of the administrator's role were voiced. Many staff members felt that the dominant thrust of Alexander's job was to be involved with staff, while he felt that his essential task was to write proposals, monitor programs, and provide resources.

As a function of this experience, adjustments were made in all areas. New communication structures were created, and Alexander spent more time with staff, while some staff members became more involved in administrative procedures. Clarity about expectations resolved people's feelings. The polarity was neutralized.

10.12   Getting Things Done Requires That Someone Does Them

In every school there are a great variety of tasks to be performed. Everything—from insuring that yard duty schedules are made, to purchasing paper clips, to all the teaching functions—needs to be done by someone. When it is not clear *who* is to do something, role ambiguity is the result.

One of the results of this problem is that some things don't get done because everyone assumes that someone else is responsible. Frustration and stress increase when people don't have the resources necessary to do their jobs. Personal conflict results from these frustrations, and blaming occurs. Role clarity—identifying who does what, when—allows you to avoid such problems.

10.13   The Difference Between Job Description and Role Clarity

A job description identifies the *functions* that need to be performed in order to fulfill a role. There are several things it does *not* define:

a. The relative importance of the different functions.
b. The manner (style) in which they are to be carried out.
c. The relative amounts of time to be devoted to each.
d. The way in which personal mannerisms affect how the functions are performed.

Often when people in an organization are disagreeing about a person's role, they are in conflict about the things the job description doesn't say.

Many school systems have quite definitive job descriptions for all personnel, but role clarity still remains a problem. For example, your job description may indicate that you are to observe teachers in your school and assist them in improving their skills. You may find that in light of all your other tasks, you have, on the average, ten minutes a week left over to do this. Some of your teachers (who need help) may feel that you're not doing your job. It is necessary, in this example, for you to assess your job priorities in the light of teacher and central office expectations.

In spite of job descriptions, if people (including yourself) place differing degrees of importance on different functions, conflict will occur.

As time passes, conditions change. A job description that fits at one time may not at some future period. Job descriptions do not usually provide the mechanics for changing the relative importance of different functions. You need not only a job description but also a "how-to-change" description; otherwise as roles change, job descriptions will become irrelevant.

10.2 WHAT IS A ROLE?

It is useful at this point to clarify some definitions.

Function—a definable task that a person performs, which can often be part of a job description. Any specific functions may have subfunctions, i.e., a reading resource teacher has as one function the diagnosing of reading problems. As a result of this, other functions, such as having meetings with teachers or other resource people, completing reports, etc., are necessary.

Role—a collection of often related functions which are given to one person to perform. The person colors the way in which the functions are performed by:

a. Deciding about the relative importance of each.
b. Determining time alloted to each.
c. Performing them in a certain style.
d. Influencing them with personal mannerisms.

Role Clarity—the degree to which the person performing the role, and others who are affected by the role, agree on the functions and how they are to be performed.

Status—the relationship of one role to another in an organizational system, especially regarding the authority that one person has to influence the performance of another. No one can perform his own role well unless others are performing theirs well.

 Role Change—a role changes when any of the following events occur:

a. Functions are added or deleted.
b. The relative importance of any function changes because of changing conditions.
c. New conditions require altering the time allotted to a function.
d. A new person assumes the role, so that style and personal mannerisms change.
e. The person performing the role changes in his view of the role.
f. Persons influenced by the role change in their perception of it.

10.3 HOW TO DETERMINE WHAT A PERSON'S ROLE IS

The following sections describe a role-clarification procedure that can be used with your staff.

10.31 Asking People What Things They Do

In a school which has 20 to 30 certificated and classified employees, it is unlikely that everyone knows completely what everyone else does. It is more likely that people will be most concerned about whether others are doing those things that help them do their own jobs. Making clear what people do has several advantages.

• When people are aware of all the things others do, they can usually be more tolerant of periodic failures in other's performance.

• It can become apparent what things need to be done, that aren't presently being done.

• Persons with closely interrelated roles can check whether each sees himself as doing things that the other needs.

10.311 A procedure for describing what things people do

• Have everyone on the staff keep an informal log for one week, in which they list the things they do with a rough estimate of the amount of time spent on each task. Include school-related tasks done outside of school hours. Many people on your staff would find the form in Figure 10-1 a help in keeping this log.

ACTIVITY LOG

Instructions:

You can use this form to record how much time during the week you spend performing certain tasks. The record will be most accurate if you take a couple of minutes during lunch and after school to list your activities and time spent on each. Include school-related activities during evening hours, e.g., classroom preparation, conference or phone calls to parents, etc.

Name _____ Position _____
From _____ To _____

	Mon.	Tues.	Wed.	Etc.
Task	Task Time	Task Time	Task Time	Etc.

FIGURE 10-1

• Be sure to emphasize to certificated staff that they should be especially aware of non-teaching functions that they perform. Make sure that classified staff include tasks in which they are involved with children.

• At a meeting devoted to this purpose, have each staff member list the results of their week's log, including percentages of work time devoted to each function during the week. They should add other functions that may be done regularly, but that were not performed during the previous week.

• Divide the staff into "job-alike" groups. Some groups may have only one member! Such job-alike groups will vary in different schools; the following list gives an idea of the possibilities:

primary teachers	administrator
intermediate teachers	resource teachers
special ed teachers	classroom aides
custodians	same grade teachers
office personnel	other ancillary personnel

• Have each job-alike group compare the task lists of its members, and make a new profile of the weekly tasks of the group.

• Have each group place its task list on large sheets of paper for display.

• Have a "gallery review" in which everyone can inspect all other lists.

• Discuss the lists in the large group, and address certain questions:

a. Are there things on other lists that you were not previously aware were done by them?

b. Are there things you assumed others did, which do not appear on their list?

c. Are you aware of things that need to be done, that don't appear on any list?

• If new features are uncovered, adjust the lists accordingly.

• If tasks not listed are uncovered, add them to a list only with the permission of the person(s) involved. Any new tasks that are not clearly anyone's responsibility should be listed separately.

• Make copies of the final products and distribute them to all staff.

10.32 Asking People with Whom They Need to Do Things

In order for everyone to perform his role effectively, others must be doing their jobs. This is especially so in a modern elementary school, where a high degree of interdependence is involved.

The ability to do the tasks one is expected to do (by oneself or others) depends on whether each person on the staff is interacting adequately and sufficiently with relevant others.

In Section 10.31, your staff was asked to list the things they do. It is important that these functions be looked at from the point of view of whom they need to be done with.

Many important functions are overlooked when people only consider their "main" functions. The tasks that are often ignored are the ones that involve the communication linkages that are necessary for people to do their jobs effectively. These functions include:

a. Meetings with others to share information.
b. Feedback reports to confirm evaluations or diagnoses.
c. Updating of information on long-term issues.
d. Record keeping that others need to know about.

10.321 A procedure for finding out with whom people need to do things

The survey instrument shown in Figure 10-2 may be used in order to illuminate where in your school important communication linkages are missing. This survey may be used as part of an overall role clarification process, or independently. You may use the job-alike groupings identified in Section 10.311 as the basis of this survey, and reconstruct it to fit your situation.

When the survey is completed you score it, especially looking for instances in which need for frequent interaction is accompanied by dissatisfaction. When several people in one category indicate dissatisfaction with another category, you have a communication problem. In any case, knowing where dissatisfaction exists gives you the opportunity to become involved with the problem.

"WHOM DO YOU NEED TO INTERACT WITH?"

On this survey form you will have an opportunity to indicate your views on communication within your school. I hope you will be candid in your responses, so that we can work toward improving our communication network.

As you will see, the form lists just about anyone in the school or district with whom you *might* need to interact in order to get your work done effectively. On the left side of the solid line, circle one number on each line that best summarizes how much you believe you need to interact with that person or group. On the right side of the solid line circle one number on each line that best fits your feelings of satisfaction or dissatisfaction with the quality and/or quantity of these interactions. I will report to you the summary of the staff's responses.

FIGURE 10-2

	Very often	Often	Some-times	Rarely	Never	AT PRESENT:		
						Very satis-fied	Gener-ally satis-fied	Dis-satis-fied
1. Grade level teachers (yours)	1	2	3	4	5	1	2	3
2. All primary teachers	1	2	3	4	5	1	2	3
3. All intermediate teachers	1	2	3	4	5	1	2	3
4. District superintendent	1	2	3	4	5	1	2	3
5. Resource teachers	1	2	3	4	5	1	2	3
6. Other district office personnel	1	2	3	4	5	1	2	3
7. Classroom aides	1	2	3	4	5	1	2	3
8. School administrator	1	2	3	4	5	1	2	3
9. The whole staff	1	2	3	4	5	1	2	3
10. Teachers from other schools	1	2	3	4	5	1	2	3
11. Psychologist	1	2	3	4	5	1	2	3
12. Curriculum specialist	1	2	3	4	5	1	2	3
13. Custodian	1	2	3	4	5	1	2	3
14. Bus drivers	1	2	3	4	5	1	2	3
15. Secretary	1	2	3	4	5	1	2	3
16. Special ed teacher	1	2	3	4	5	1	2	3
17. Other: _____	1	2	3	4	5	1	2	3
18. Other: _____	1	2	3	4	5	1	2	3

FIGURE 10-2 *(continued)*

10.33 Asking People What They Need from Others in Order to Do Their Job

Knowing about the need for interaction among different roles in the school answers only part of the problem of role clarification. You still need to know what people need from each other, so that expectations can be further clarified.

In order for people to do their jobs, they need one or more of the following things from others:

a. Material resources
b. Information
c. Decisions
d. Activities

10.331 A procedure for determining what people need from each other

Use the reference groups that have been used in previous sections of this chapter as a starting point. You may also use any other method for sorting out discriminable roles, i.e., the problem communication linkages defined in Section 10.32, or other conflicts within the staff.

• Define the roles to be addressed in this process.

• Divide the participants into small groups according to roles.

• Ask all groups or individuals to consider what they need from the others in order to do their job.

• Describe the four areas to which they should address themselves, i.e., material resources, information, decision, and activities, as specifically as possible.

  a. Material resources: money, paper, books, learning materials, etc.
  b. Information: clarification of policies and rules; data about children, beliefs, and attitudes; information about what people are doing; norms and expectations; and any other kind of information that would be helpful in accomplishing one's work.
  c. Decisions: How others make decisions that affect one's own role; what decisions one can make in reference to another's work; who is responsible for different types of decisions; what decisions have been made.
  d. Activities: What do other people do, and how does it affect others? What do others need to do so that one can do one's job?

• Have each role group or individual place the results of the above procedure on large sheets of paper and provide time for a "gallery review."

• All members of the staff now have an opportunity to see what others expect of them, and the full range of needs that exist between roles in the school.

• Transcribe the material from the large sheets, and distribute the final document to all staff.

10.34 Asking People About the Degree to Which They Can Fulfill Other's Expectations

The procedures outlined in Section 10.331 delineate the expectations that exist between roles within the school. Problems arise when there is little clarity about the degree to which expectations can be fulfilled. Mrs. Jones expects Mr. Smith to do something she needs, but Mr. Smith cannot do it because of circumstances beyond his control. Mrs. Jones is not aware of the circumstances, so attributes Mr. Smith's lack of performance to laziness, bad will, or incompetence. Blaming and conflict ensue.

The final step in role clarification is to assess the degree to which people's expectations can be reasonably fulfilled. If this is not done, people will continue to have unmet needs without knowing why they aren't being met.

10.341 A procedure for clarifying the degree to which expectations can be fulfilled

As a function of the procedure completed in Section 10.331, all persons filling a role, or "job-alike" groups in the school, have a list of what others expect of them. In order to complete the process of clarifying roles and expectations, the following steps need to be taken:
- Have each role (group) look at the list of things that are expected of them.
- Each expectation should be evaluated, initially, in terms of whether it is understandable. Any statements that are *unclear* should be noted.
- Those statements that are understandable should be rated in the following manner:

  1 - I (we) can do this, and have been or will begin doing this.
  2 - I (we) can do this, but only under certain conditions.
  3 - I (we) cannot foresee being able to do this.

- Have people representing each role that has been evaluated in this process meet together as a group, observed by the rest of the staff. It is useful during the ensuing discussion if time is given periodically for the representatives to meet with those they represent to discuss progress.
- Starting with any role, have that person go over the list of expectations, indicating his evaluation of the statement. Any statement rated as 2 should be discussed to ascertain whether the conditions necessary for fulfilling it can be effected. Statements rated as 3 should also be discussed. Often "3" ratings arise from a lack of clarity, which the discussion can clarify. Major conflicts that emerge and that seem not to be resolvable at this time can be given to a task force (described below). Unclear expectations should be explained by the group that made them.
- Have a recorder make notes of the way each expectation is resolved.
- Upon the conclusion of this process (which may take two or more meetings, depending on the size of your staff), all staff members will have a much clearer understanding of the roles of all other members of the staff.
- A document which results from this procedure should be completed and distributed to all staff.
- A task force should be selected from the staff to meet at a future time to look at the major conflicts that were not resolved through this process and to develop proposals to the staff for resolving them.

10.4 CHANGING ROLES

In the one-room schoolhouse of the last century, role clarification was not a critical educational problem. In the modern elementary school, it is a perennial issue. New programs, new kinds of personnel, unionization, changing public expectations—all contribute to affecting what people do. Under changing circumstances the "role of the school" is a pressing philosophical issue; confusion about the roles of personnel within the school is a result.

As more people become involved in your school—parents, aides, specialists—the roles of teachers and administrators change. People have been trained to undertake some functions, but not others. In effect, the personnel within our schools must continually retrain themselves in order to keep pace with new functions.

The administrator will be looked to not only for educational leadership in the traditional sense, but also for leadership in redefining and restructuring the roles and responsibilities within his or her school. The knowledge of effective processes for doing this will permit change to be the occasion for exploring new possibilities—for teachers as well as for children.

Bibliography

The authors have found the following list of books and articles useful in their work with schools. Many of the books that are listed have extensive references which do not need to be repeated in this work. Asterisks denote those works that a school administrator will find worthwhile to include in his own professional library.

The referenced works are for those who wish to make further exploration than this Handbook presents.

CHAPTER 1

*Fox, R. S., Schmuck, R., Van Egmond, E., Ritva, M., and Jung, C., *Diagnosing Professional Climate of Schools*. NTL Learning Resources Corp., Inc., 2817-N Dorr Ave., Fairfax, Virginia 22030, 1973.

Halpin, A. W. and Croft, D. B., *The Organizational Climate of Schools*. Chicago: The University of Chicago, 1963.

Herman, J. J., *Developing an Effective School Staff Evaluation Program*. West Nyack: Parker Publishing Co., Inc., 1973.

Moos, R., *The Social Climate Scales: An Overview*. Palo Alto: Consulting Psychologists Press, 1974.

Moos, R. H., *Evaluating Treatment Environments: A Social Ecological Approach*. New York: John Wiley and Sons, Inc., 1974.

*Wick, J. W. and Beggs, D. L., *Evaluation for Decision Making in the Schools*. New York: Houghton Mifflin Co., 1971.

CHAPTER 2

Hall, J., "Decisions—Decisions—Decisions," *Psychology Today*, November, 1971.

Pfeiffer, J. W. and Jones, J. E., *Annual Handbook for Group Facilitators*. University Associates Publishers, Inc., 7596 Eads Avenue, La Jolla, California 92037.

*Schmuck, R. A., Runkel, P. J., et. al., *Handbook of Organizational Development in Schools*. National Press Books, 850 Hansen Way, Palo Alto, California 94304, 1972.

CHAPTER 3

Marshall, H. H., *Positive Discipline and Classroom Interaction: A Part of the Teaching-Learning Process*. Springfield: Charles C. Thomas, Publisher, 1972.

Chernow F. and Chernow, C., *School Administrator's Guide to Managing People*. West Nyack: Parker Publishing Co., Inc., 1976.

Clemes, H. and Bean, R., *Setting Limits and Rules for Children: A Manual of Discipline*. APOD Publications, 1427 Forty-First Avenue, Capitola, California 95010, 1976.

Howard, E. R. and Brainard, E. A., *How School Administrators Make Things Happen*. West Nyack: Parker Publishing Co., Inc. 1975.

Organizational Development in Schools, ed. by R. A. Schmuck and M. B. Miles, National Press Books, 850 Hansen Way, Palo Alto, California 94304, 1971.

Schmuck and Runkel, op. cit.

Welch, D. I. and Schutte, W., *Discipline: A Shared Experience*. Shields Publishing Co., Inc., Fort Collins, Colorado 80521, 1973.

CHAPTER 4

Bach, G. R. and Wyden, P., *The Intimate Enemy: How to Fight Fair in Love and Marriage*. New York: William Morrow and Co., Inc., 1969.

Derr, C. B., "Conflict Resolution in Organizations: View from the Field of Educational Administration," *Public Administration Review*. Sept./ Oct., 1972.

James, H. and Jongeward, D., *Born to Win: Transactional Analysis with Gestalt Experiments*. Reading: Addison-Wesley Publishing Co., 1971.

Schmuck and Miles, op. cit.

Watzlawick, P., Weakland, J., and Fisch, R., *Change: Principles of Problem Formation and Problem Resolution*. New York: W. W. Norton and Co., Inc., 1974.

CHAPTER 5

*Likert, R., *The Human Organization: Its Management and Value*. New York: McGraw-Hill Book Co., 1967.

*Schmuck, R. A. and Schmuck, P. A., *Group Processes in the Classroom* (from series: *Issues and Innovations in Education*). Dubuque: Wm. C. Brown Co., 1971.

Change in School Systems, ed. by Goodwin Watson, National Training Laboratories, N.E.A., 1967.

CHAPTER 6

Antolini, R., Levy, R., and Urban, N., Dissertation: "Belonging, Uniqueness, Personal Control, Values: The Enhancement of a Child's Self-Esteem through the Development and Use of a Teacher's Observation Tool, a Child Self-Report, and Specific Classroom Activities," School of Education, University of San Francisco, April, 1975.

*Bean, R., and Clemes, H., *The Four Conditions of Self-Esteem: A New Approach for Elementary Classrooms*. APOD Publications, Capitola, California 95010, 1977.

*Canfield, J., and Wells, H. C., *100 Ways to Enhance Self-Concept in the Classroom: A Handbook for Teachers and Parents* (from Prentice-Hall Curriculum and Teaching Series). Englewood Ciffs: Prentice-Hall, Inc., 1976.

*Coopersmith, S., *The Antecedents of Self-Esteem*. San Francisco: W. H. Freeman and Co., 1967.

*Purkey, W. W., *Self-Concept and School Achievement*. Englewood Cliffs: Prentice-Hall, Inc., 1970.

*Simon, S. B., Howe, L., and Kirschenbaum, H., *Values Clarification: A Handbook of Practical Strategies for Teachers and Students*. New York: Hart Publishing Co., Inc., 1972.

CHAPTER 7

Clemes, H. and Bean, R., *The Manresa Family Counseling Program: A Report*, Santa Cruz County Office of Education, Richard R. Fickel, Superintendent, Santa Cruz, California 95060, 1972.

Greenwood, G. E., Breivogeland, W. F., and Bessent, H., "Some Promising Approaches to Parent Involvement," *Theory Into Practice*, June 1972.

Shalvey, D., *LEAP: Language Enhancement Augmented with Parents*, Title I—Exemplary Project, Merced City School District, 444 West 23rd St., Merced, California 95340.

CHAPTER 8

Boy, A. U. and Pine, G. J., *Expanding the Self: Personal Growth for Teachers* (from series: *Issues and Innovations in Education*). Dubuque: Wm. C. Brown Co., 1971.

Fensterheim, H. and Baer, J., *Don't Say Yes When You Want to Say No*. New York: Dell Publishing Co., Inc., 1975.

Geba, B. H., *Breath Away Your Tensions*. New York and Berkeley: Random House/Bookworks, 1973.

*Lakein, A., *How to Get Control of Your Time and Your Life*. New York: Signet Book, New American Library, 1973.

Mahoney, M. J. and Thoreson, C. E., *Self-Control: Power to the Person*. Brooks/Cole Publishing Co., Monterey, California, 1974.

Progoff, Ira, *At a Journal Workshop: The Basic Text and Guide for Using the Intensive Journal*. Dialogue House Library, 45 West Tenth St., New York 10011, 1975.

Samuels, M., and Bennett, H., *The Well Body Book*. New York and Berkeley: Random House/Bookworks, 1973.

*Samuels, M., and Samuels, N., *Seeing with the Mind's Eye: The History, Techniques and Uses of Visualization*. New York and Berkeley: Random House/Bookworks, 1975.

Smith, M. J., *When I Say No, I Feel Guilty: How to Cope–Using the Skills of Systematic Assertive Therapy*. New York: The Dial Press, 1975.

Walker, C. E., *Learn to Relax*, Englewood Cliffs: Prentice-Hall, Inc., 1975.

CHAPTER 9

Johnson, D. W., *Reaching Out: Interpersonal Effectiveness and Self-Actualization*. Englewood Cliffs: Prentice-Hall, Inc., 1972.

*Satir, V., *Peoplemaking*, Palo Alto: Science and Behavior Books, 1972.

Timmins, L., *Understanding Through Communication: Structured Experiments in Self-Exploration*. Springfield: Charles C. Thomas, Publisher, 1972.

CHAPTER 10

Kahn, R. L., Wolfe, Quinn, and Snoek, *Organizational Stress: Studies in Conflict and Ambiguity*. New York: John Wiley and Sons, Inc., 1964.

Telfer, R. G., "Differentiation: A Means For Improving Staff Utilization," *Clearing House*, Oct., 1971.

Index